image comics presents

THE WALKING DEAD

™

D1400654

ROBERT KIRKMAN
CREATOR, WRITER, LETTERER

CHARLIE ADLARD
PENCILER, INKER

CLIFF RATHBURN
GRAY TONES

TONY MOORE
COVER

for image comics:

Erik Larsen
Publisher

Marc Silvestri
CEO

Todd McFarlane
President

Jim Valentino
Vice-President

Eric Stephenson
Executive Director

Brett Evans
Production Manager

Cindie Espinoza
Controller

B. Clay Moore
PR & Marketing Coordinator

Jon Malin
Production Assistant

Tim Hegarty
Booktrade/Intl. Rights

Allen Hui
Web Developer

THE WALKING DEAD, VOL. 2: MILES BEHIND US. October, 2004. First Printing. Published by Image Comics, Inc. Office of Publication: 1071 N. Batavia St. Suite A, Orange, CA 92867. Image and its logos are ® and © 2004, Image Comics, Inc. All Rights Reserved. THE WALKING DEAD is ™ and © 2004, Robert Kirkman. Originally published in single magazine format as THE WALKING DEAD #7-12. The story and characters presented in this publication are fictional. Any similarities to events or persons living or dead is purely coincidental. With the exception of artwork used for review purposes, none of the contents here in may be reproduced without the expressed written permission of the copyright holder.
PRINTED IN USA

www.imagecomics.com

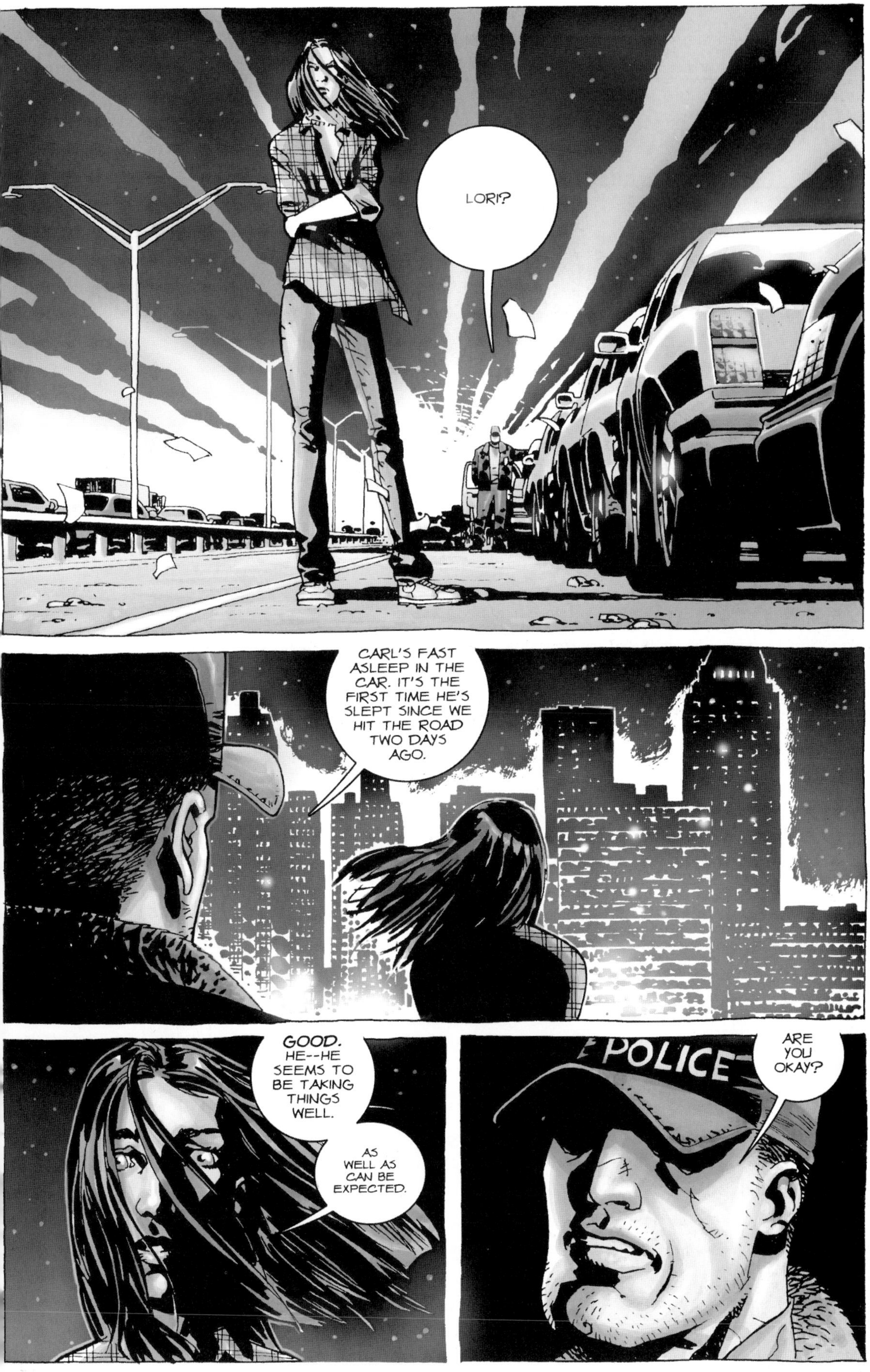
LORI?
CARL'S FAST ASLEEP IN THE CAR. IT'S THE FIRST TIME HE'S SLEPT SINCE WE HIT THE ROAD TWO DAYS AGO.
GOOD. HE--HE SEEMS TO BE TAKING THINGS WELL.
AS WELL AS CAN BE EXPECTED.
POLICE
ARE YOU OKAY?

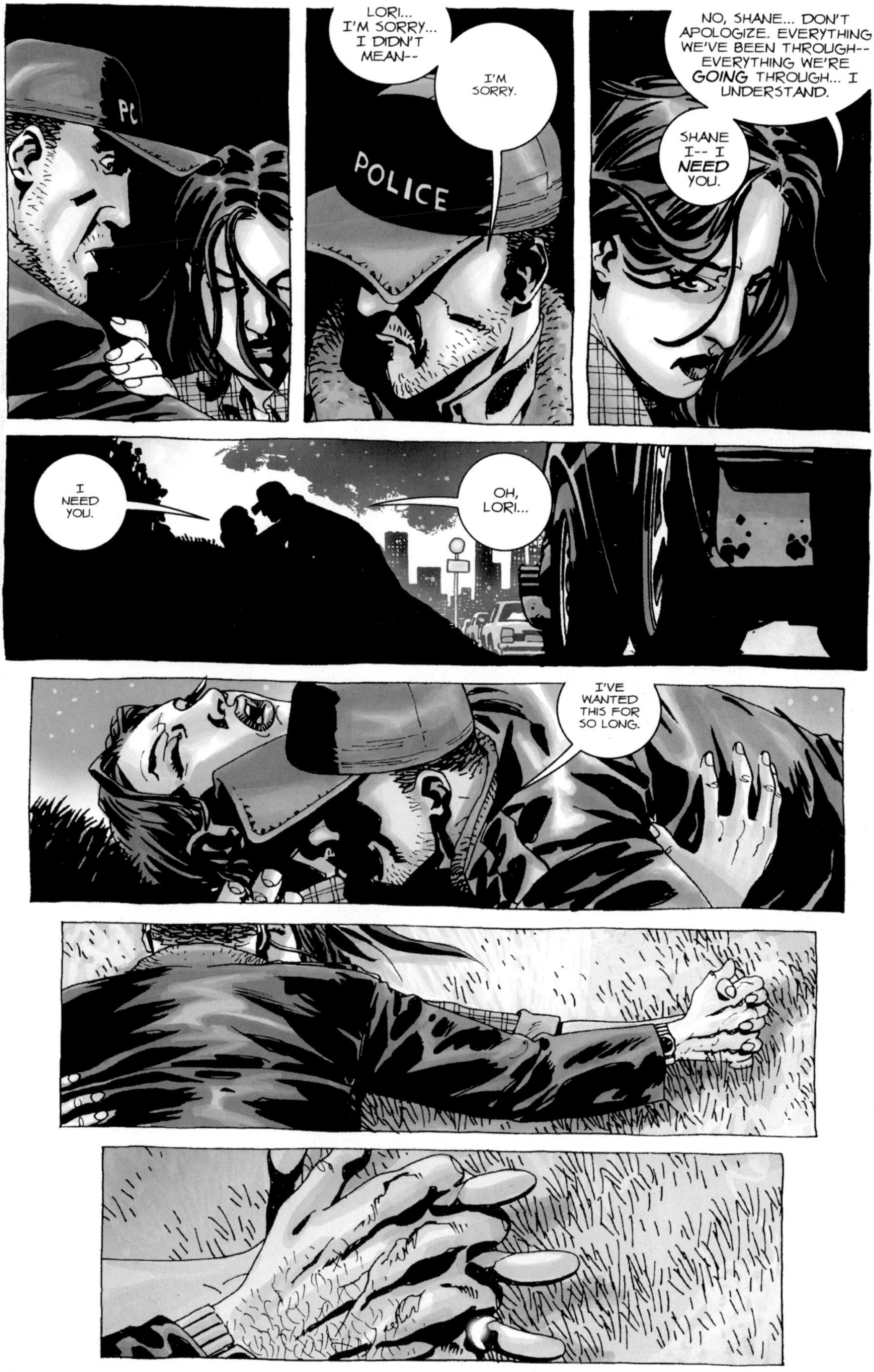

LORI... I'M SORRY... I DIDN'T MEAN--
I'M SORRY.
NO, SHANE... DON'T APOLOGIZE. EVERYTHING WE'VE BEEN THROUGH-- EVERYTHING WE'RE **GOING** THROUGH... I UNDERSTAND.
SHANE I-- I **NEED** YOU.
I NEED YOU.
OH, LORI...
I'VE WANTED THIS FOR SO LONG.

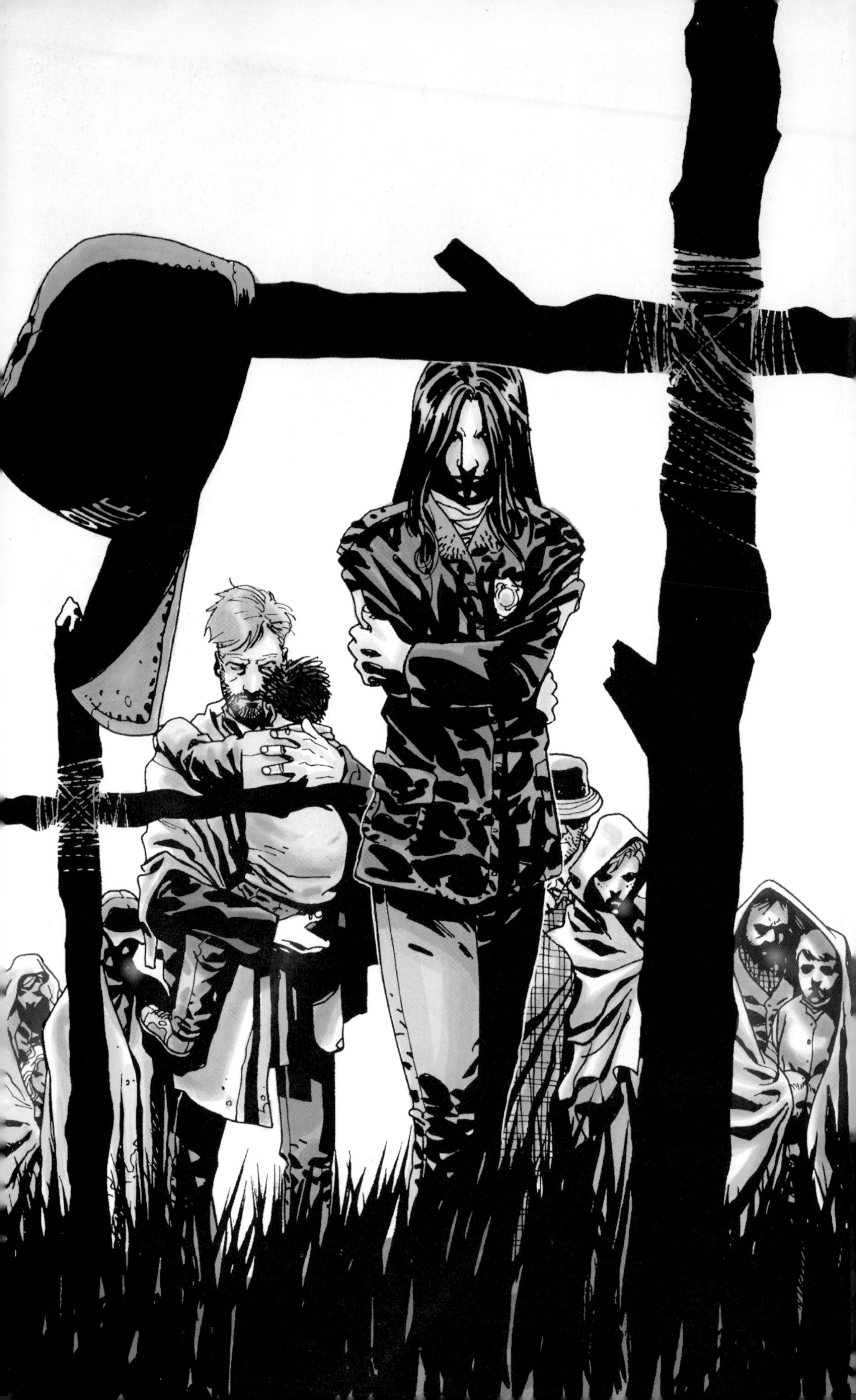

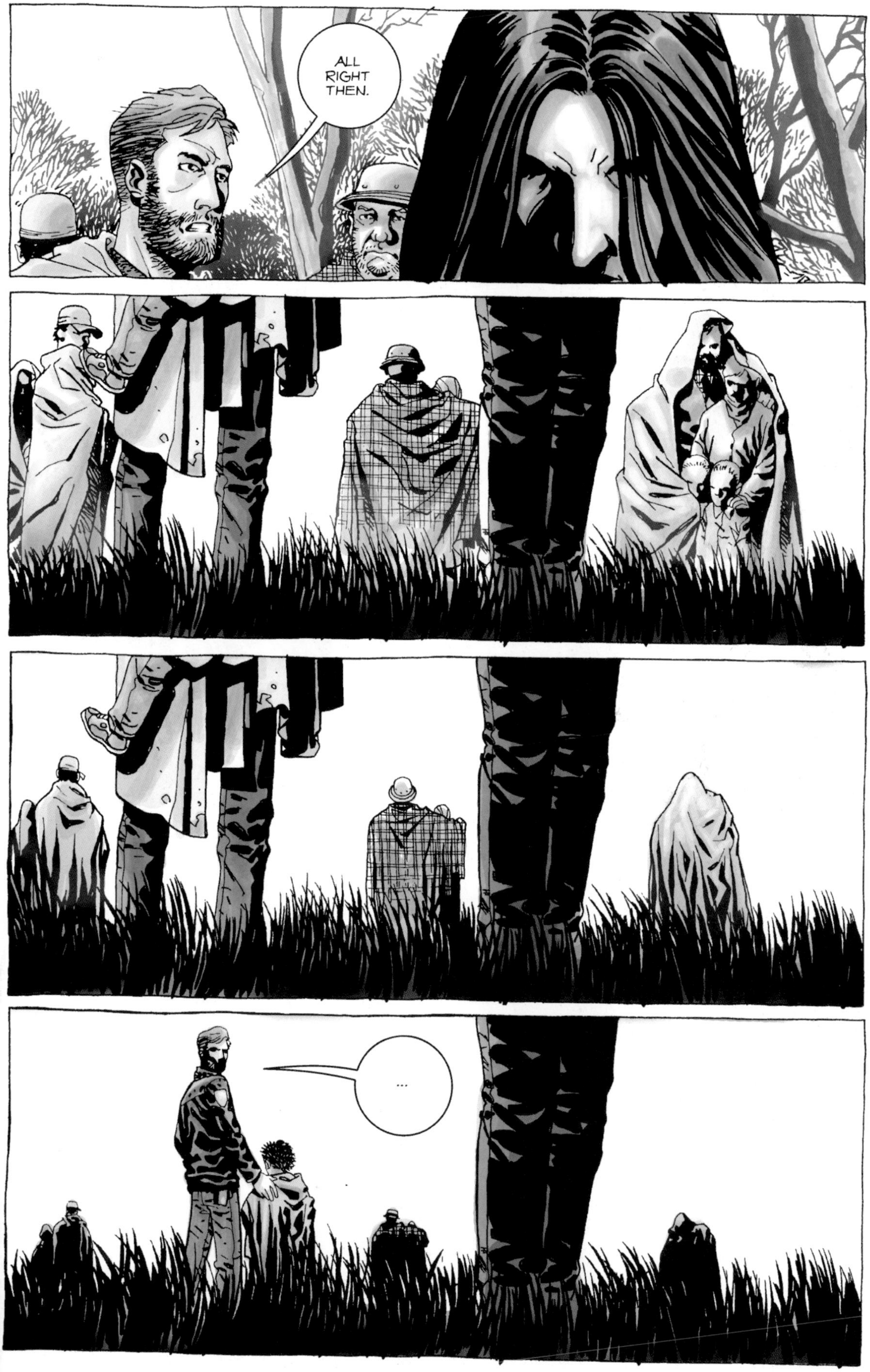
ALL RIGHT THEN.
...

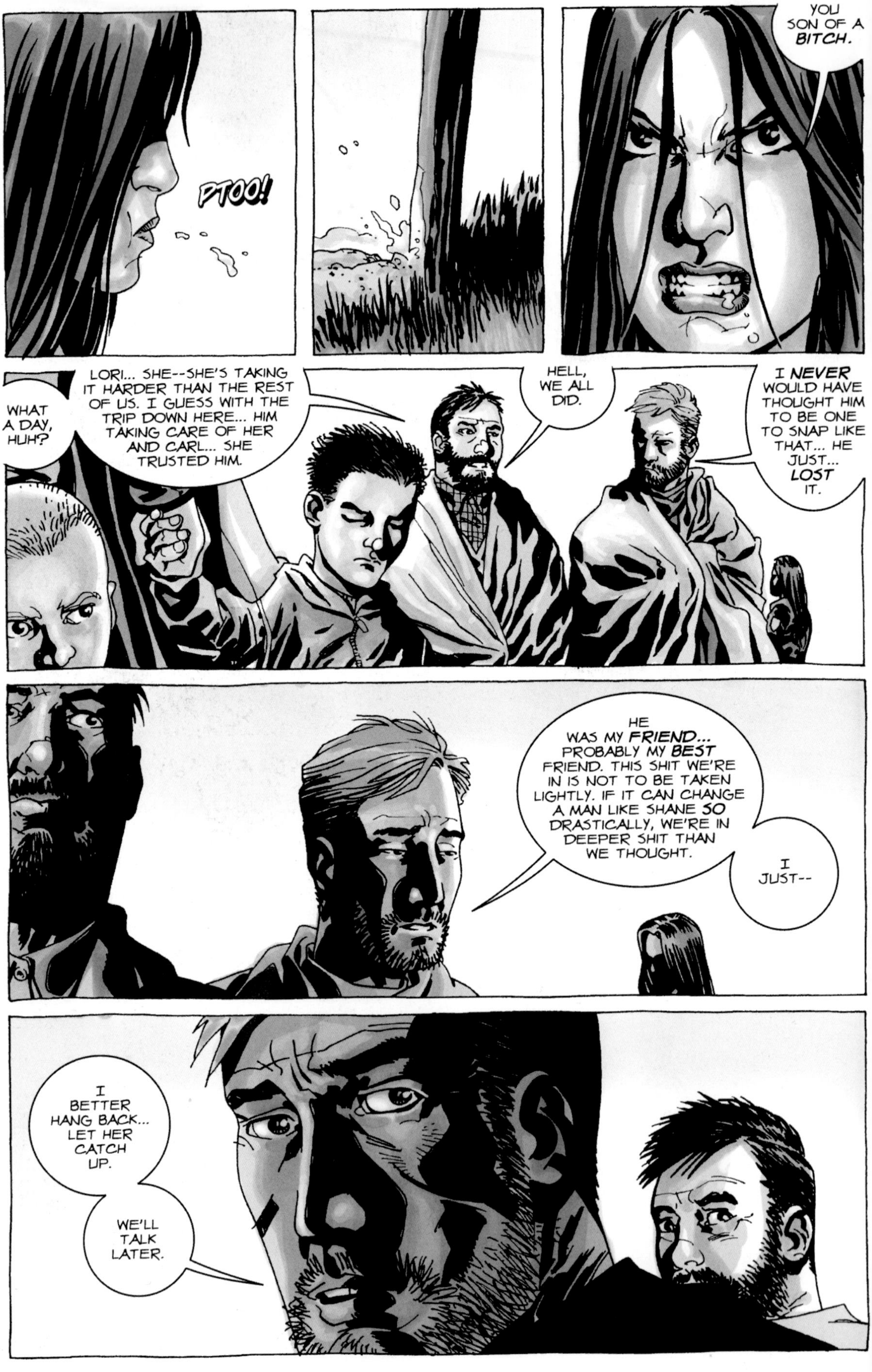
PTOO!
YOU SON OF A BITCH.
WHAT A DAY, HUH?
LORI... SHE--SHE'S TAKING IT HARDER THAN THE REST OF US. I GUESS WITH THE TRIP DOWN HERE... HIM TAKING CARE OF HER AND CARL... SHE TRUSTED HIM.
HELL, WE ALL DID.
I NEVER WOULD HAVE THOUGHT HIM TO BE ONE TO SNAP LIKE THAT... HE JUST... LOST IT.
HE WAS MY FRIEND... PROBABLY MY BEST FRIEND. THIS SHIT WE'RE IN IS NOT TO BE TAKEN LIGHTLY. IF IT CAN CHANGE A MAN LIKE SHANE SO DRASTICALLY, WE'RE IN DEEPER SHIT THAN WE THOUGHT.
I JUST--
I BETTER HANG BACK... LET HER CATCH UP.
WE'LL TALK LATER.

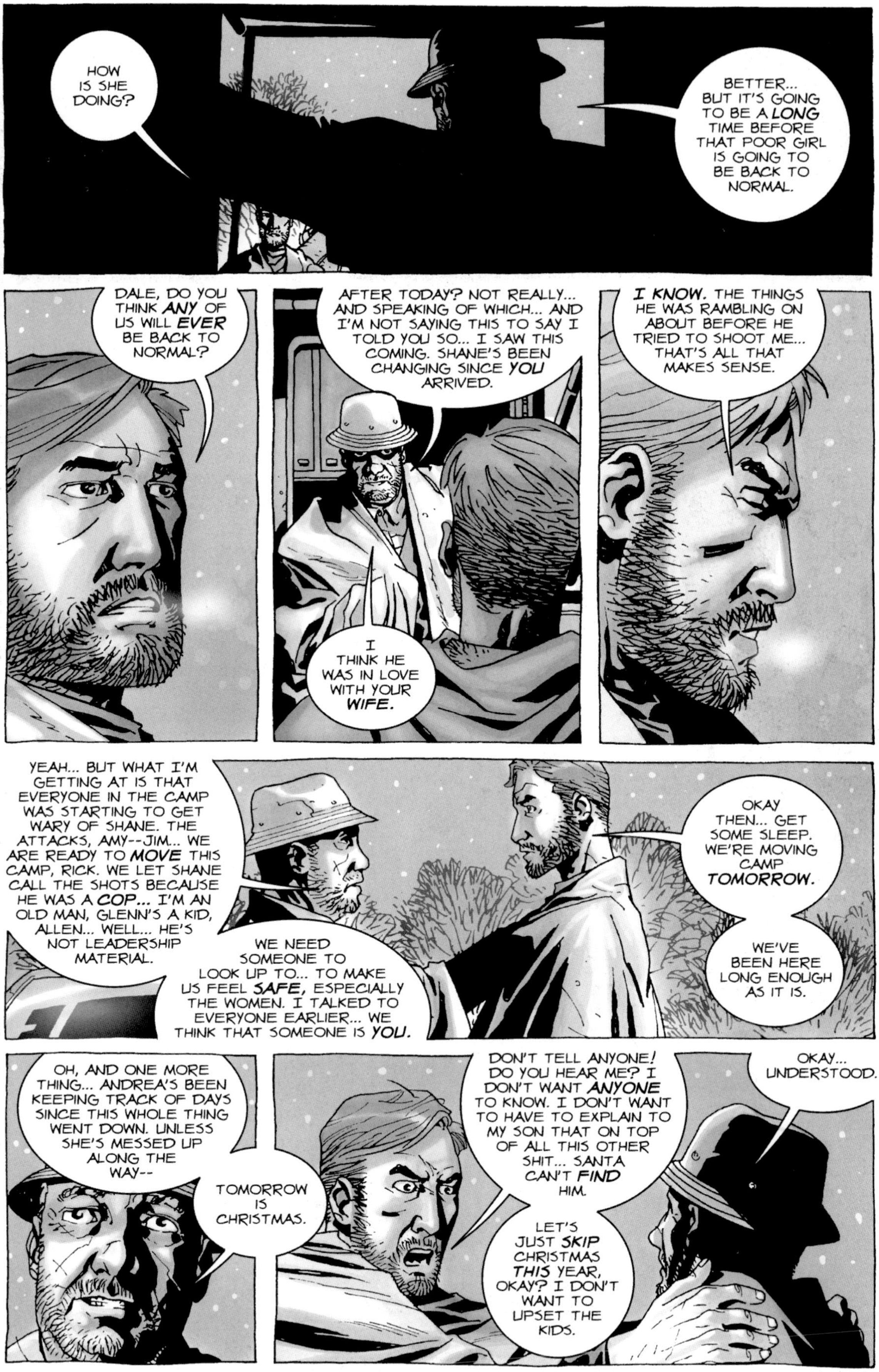
HOW IS SHE DOING?
BETTER... BUT IT'S GOING TO BE A LONG TIME BEFORE THAT POOR GIRL IS GOING TO BE BACK TO NORMAL.
DALE, DO YOU THINK ANY OF US WILL EVER BE BACK TO NORMAL?
AFTER TODAY? NOT REALLY... AND SPEAKING OF WHICH... AND I'M NOT SAYING THIS TO SAY I TOLD YOU SO... I SAW THIS COMING. SHANE'S BEEN CHANGING SINCE YOU ARRIVED.
I THINK HE WAS IN LOVE WITH YOUR WIFE.
I KNOW. THE THINGS HE WAS RAMBLING ON ABOUT BEFORE HE TRIED TO SHOOT ME... THAT'S ALL THAT MAKES SENSE.
YEAH... BUT WHAT I'M GETTING AT IS THAT EVERYONE IN THE CAMP WAS STARTING TO GET WARY OF SHANE. THE ATTACKS, AMY--JIM... WE ARE READY TO MOVE THIS CAMP, RICK. WE LET SHANE CALL THE SHOTS BECAUSE HE WAS A COP... I'M AN OLD MAN, GLENN'S A KID, ALLEN... WELL... HE'S NOT LEADERSHIP MATERIAL.
WE NEED SOMEONE TO LOOK UP TO... TO MAKE US FEEL SAFE, ESPECIALLY THE WOMEN. I TALKED TO EVERYONE EARLIER... WE THINK THAT SOMEONE IS YOU.
OKAY THEN... GET SOME SLEEP. WE'RE MOVING CAMP TOMORROW.
WE'VE BEEN HERE LONG ENOUGH AS IT IS.
OH, AND ONE MORE THING... ANDREA'S BEEN KEEPING TRACK OF DAYS SINCE THIS WHOLE THING WENT DOWN. UNLESS SHE'S MESSED UP ALONG THE WAY--
TOMORROW IS CHRISTMAS.
DON'T TELL ANYONE! DO YOU HEAR ME? I DON'T WANT ANYONE TO KNOW. I DON'T WANT TO HAVE TO EXPLAIN TO MY SON THAT ON TOP OF ALL THIS OTHER SHIT... SANTA CAN'T FIND HIM.
LET'S JUST SKIP CHRISTMAS THIS YEAR, OKAY? I DON'T WANT TO UPSET THE KIDS.
OKAY... UNDERSTOOD.

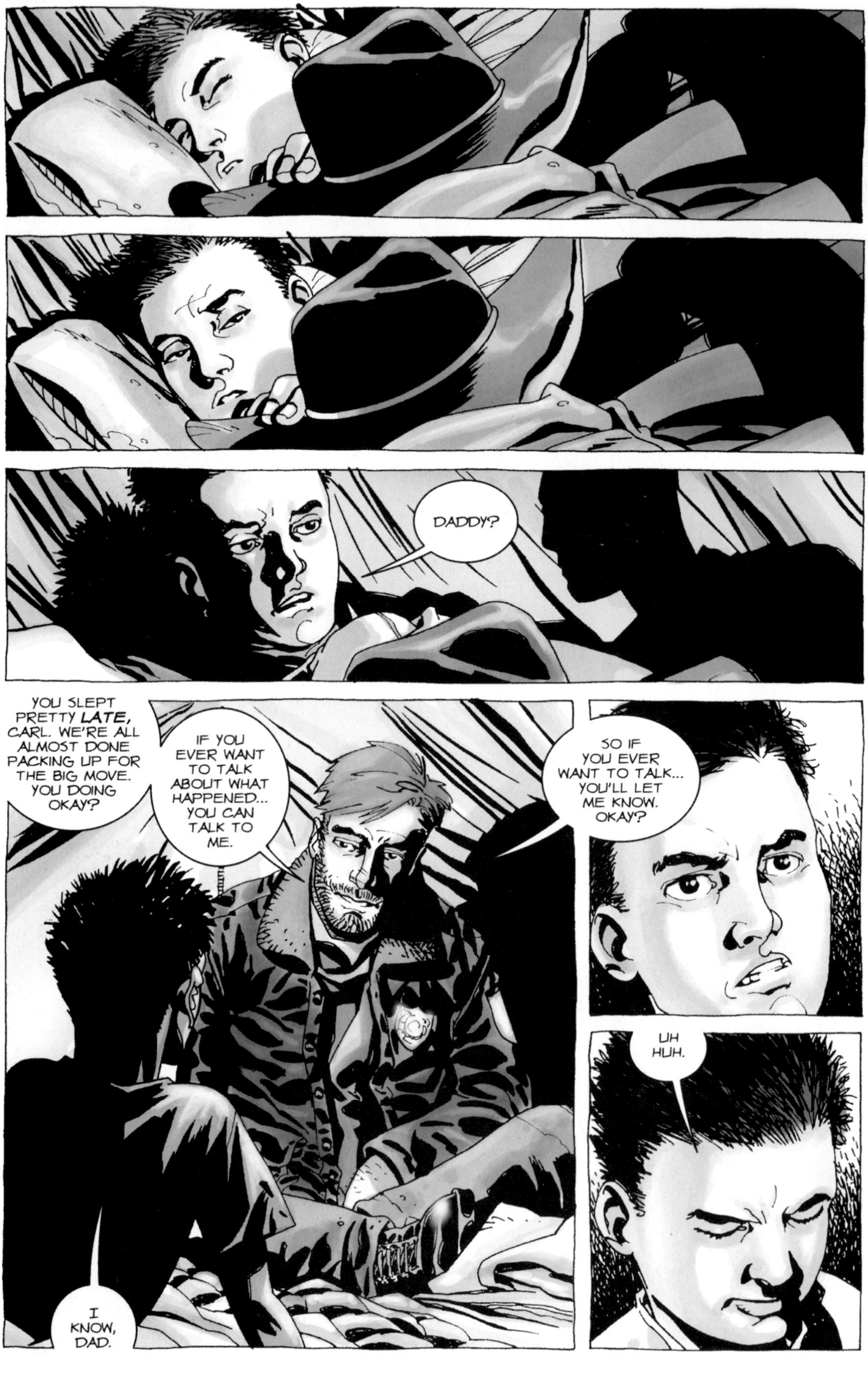
DADDY?
YOU SLEPT PRETTY **LATE,** CARL. WE'RE ALL ALMOST DONE PACKING UP FOR THE BIG MOVE. YOU DOING OKAY?
IF YOU EVER WANT TO TALK ABOUT WHAT HAPPENED... YOU CAN TALK TO ME.
I KNOW, DAD.
SO IF YOU EVER WANT TO TALK... YOU'LL LET ME KNOW. OKAY?
UH HUH.

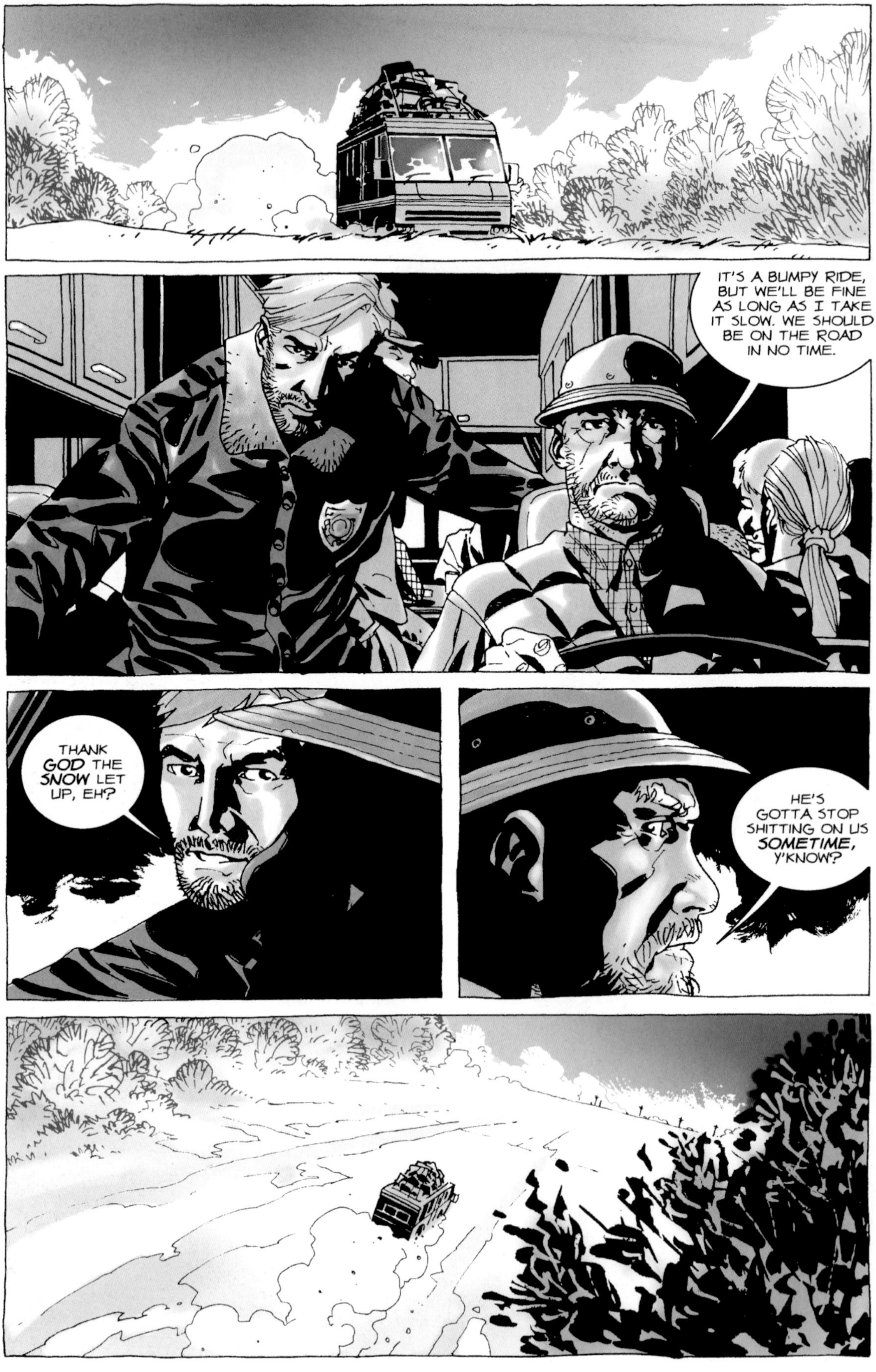
IT'S A BUMPY RIDE, BUT WE'LL BE FINE AS LONG AS I TAKE IT SLOW. WE SHOULD BE ON THE ROAD IN NO TIME.
THANK GOD THE SNOW LET UP, EH?
HE'S GOTTA STOP SHITTING ON US SOMETIME, Y'KNOW?

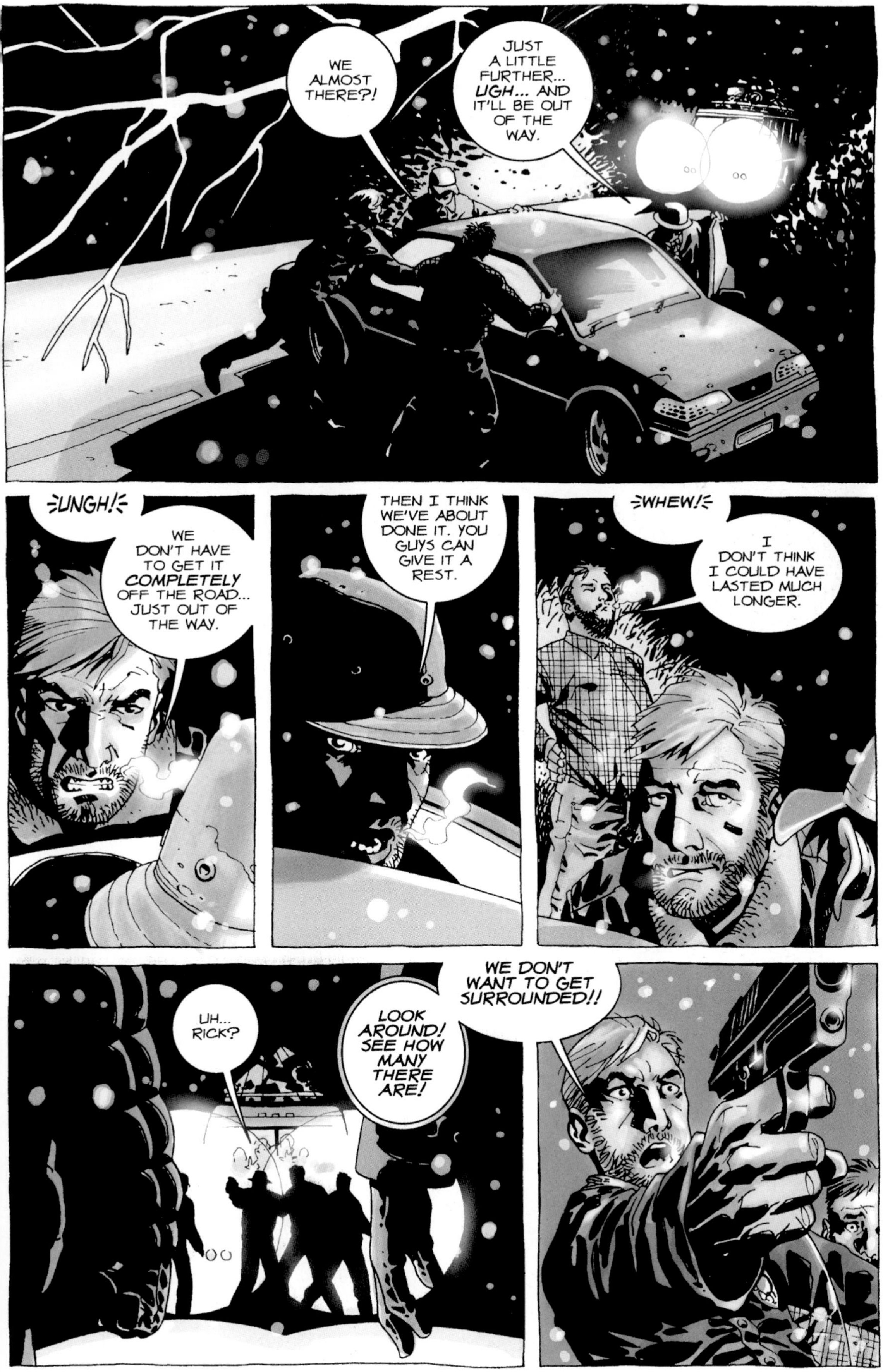
WE ALMOST THERE?!
JUST A LITTLE FURTHER... UGH... AND IT'LL BE OUT OF THE WAY.
UNGH!
WE DON'T HAVE TO GET IT COMPLETELY OFF THE ROAD... JUST OUT OF THE WAY.
THEN I THINK WE'VE ABOUT DONE IT. YOU GUYS CAN GIVE IT A REST.
WHEW!
I DON'T THINK I COULD HAVE LASTED MUCH LONGER.
UH... RICK?
LOOK AROUND! SEE HOW MANY THERE ARE!
WE DON'T WANT TO GET SURROUNDED!!

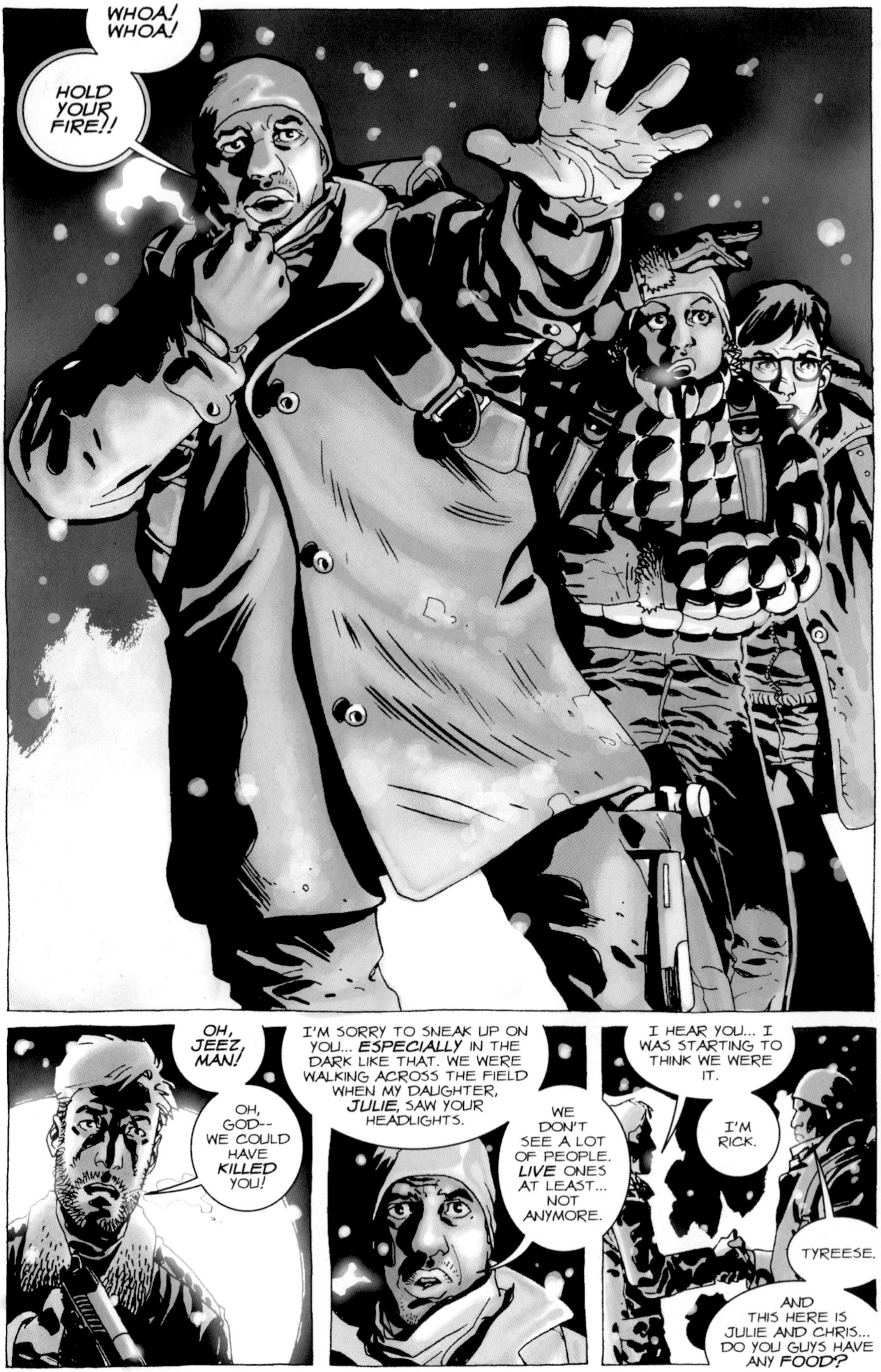

WHOA! WHOA!
HOLD YOUR FIRE!!
OH, JEEZ, MAN!
OH, GOD-- WE COULD HAVE KILLED YOU!
I'M SORRY TO SNEAK UP ON YOU... ESPECIALLY IN THE DARK LIKE THAT. WE WERE WALKING ACROSS THE FIELD WHEN MY DAUGHTER, JULIE, SAW YOUR HEADLIGHTS.
WE DON'T SEE A LOT OF PEOPLE. LIVE ONES AT LEAST... NOT ANYMORE.
I HEAR YOU... I WAS STARTING TO THINK WE WERE IT.
I'M RICK.
TYREESE.
AND THIS HERE IS JULIE AND CHRIS... DO YOU GUYS HAVE ANY FOOD?

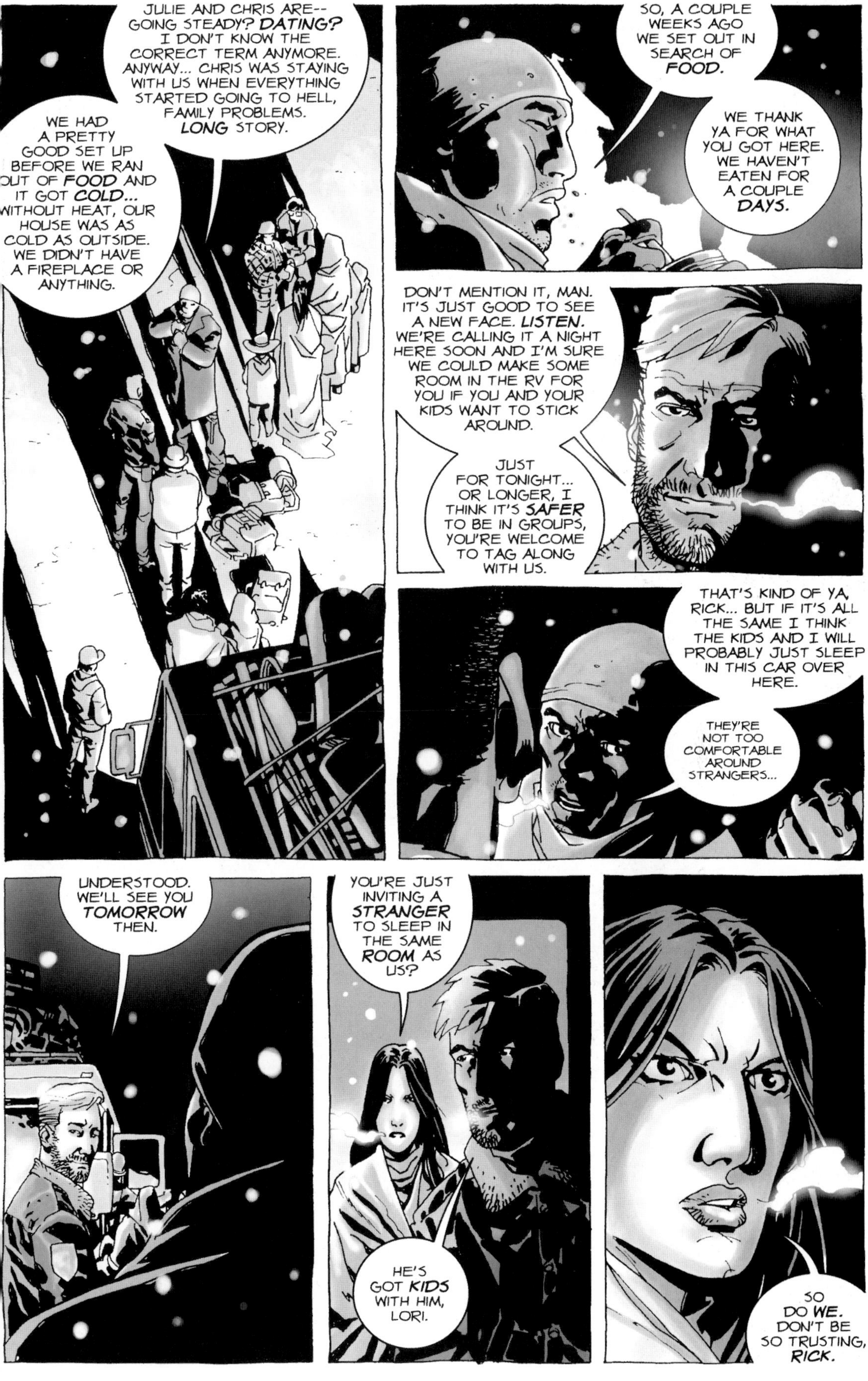
JULIE AND CHRIS ARE-- GOING STEADY? DATING? I DON'T KNOW THE CORRECT TERM ANYMORE. ANYWAY... CHRIS WAS STAYING WITH US WHEN EVERYTHING STARTED GOING TO HELL, FAMILY PROBLEMS. LONG STORY.
WE HAD A PRETTY GOOD SET UP BEFORE WE RAN OUT OF FOOD AND IT GOT COLD... WITHOUT HEAT, OUR HOUSE WAS AS COLD AS OUTSIDE. WE DIDN'T HAVE A FIREPLACE OR ANYTHING.
SO, A COUPLE WEEKS AGO WE SET OUT IN SEARCH OF FOOD.
WE THANK YA FOR WHAT YOU GOT HERE. WE HAVEN'T EATEN FOR A COUPLE DAYS.
DON'T MENTION IT, MAN. IT'S JUST GOOD TO SEE A NEW FACE. LISTEN. WE'RE CALLING IT A NIGHT HERE SOON AND I'M SURE WE COULD MAKE SOME ROOM IN THE RV FOR YOU IF YOU AND YOUR KIDS WANT TO STICK AROUND.
JUST FOR TONIGHT... OR LONGER, I THINK IT'S SAFER TO BE IN GROUPS, YOU'RE WELCOME TO TAG ALONG WITH US.
THAT'S KIND OF YA, RICK... BUT IF IT'S ALL THE SAME I THINK THE KIDS AND I WILL PROBABLY JUST SLEEP IN THIS CAR OVER HERE.
THEY'RE NOT TOO COMFORTABLE AROUND STRANGERS...
UNDERSTOOD. WE'LL SEE YOU TOMORROW THEN.
YOU'RE JUST INVITING A STRANGER TO SLEEP IN THE SAME ROOM AS US?
HE'S GOT KIDS WITH HIM, LORI.
SO DO WE. DON'T BE SO TRUSTING, RICK.

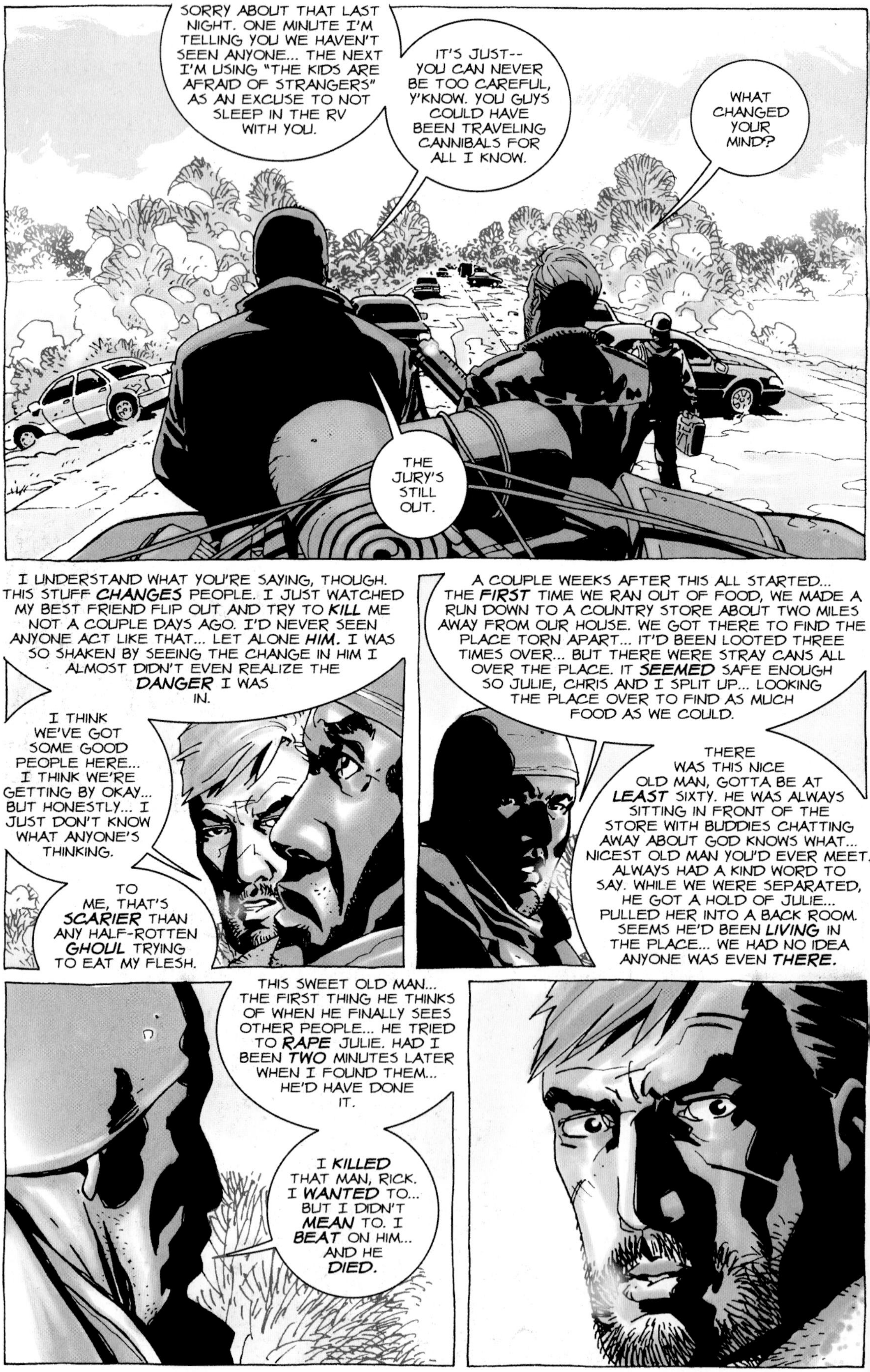
SORRY ABOUT THAT LAST NIGHT. ONE MINUTE I'M TELLING YOU WE HAVEN'T SEEN ANYONE... THE NEXT I'M USING "THE KIDS ARE AFRAID OF STRANGERS" AS AN EXCUSE TO NOT SLEEP IN THE RV WITH YOU.
IT'S JUST-- YOU CAN NEVER BE TOO CAREFUL, Y'KNOW. YOU GUYS COULD HAVE BEEN TRAVELING CANNIBALS FOR ALL I KNOW.
WHAT CHANGED YOUR MIND?
THE JURY'S STILL OUT.
I UNDERSTAND WHAT YOU'RE SAYING, THOUGH. THIS STUFF CHANGES PEOPLE. I JUST WATCHED MY BEST FRIEND FLIP OUT AND TRY TO KILL ME NOT A COUPLE DAYS AGO. I'D NEVER SEEN ANYONE ACT LIKE THAT... LET ALONE HIM. I WAS SO SHAKEN BY SEEING THE CHANGE IN HIM I ALMOST DIDN'T EVEN REALIZE THE DANGER I WAS IN.
I THINK WE'VE GOT SOME GOOD PEOPLE HERE... I THINK WE'RE GETTING BY OKAY... BUT HONESTLY... I JUST DON'T KNOW WHAT ANYONE'S THINKING.
TO ME, THAT'S SCARIER THAN ANY HALF-ROTTEN GHOUL TRYING TO EAT MY FLESH.
A COUPLE WEEKS AFTER THIS ALL STARTED... THE FIRST TIME WE RAN OUT OF FOOD, WE MADE A RUN DOWN TO A COUNTRY STORE ABOUT TWO MILES AWAY FROM OUR HOUSE. WE GOT THERE TO FIND THE PLACE TORN APART... IT'D BEEN LOOTED THREE TIMES OVER... BUT THERE WERE STRAY CANS ALL OVER THE PLACE. IT SEEMED SAFE ENOUGH SO JULIE, CHRIS AND I SPLIT UP... LOOKING THE PLACE OVER TO FIND AS MUCH FOOD AS WE COULD.
THERE WAS THIS NICE OLD MAN, GOTTA BE AT LEAST SIXTY. HE WAS ALWAYS SITTING IN FRONT OF THE STORE WITH BUDDIES CHATTING AWAY ABOUT GOD KNOWS WHAT... NICEST OLD MAN YOU'D EVER MEET. ALWAYS HAD A KIND WORD TO SAY. WHILE WE WERE SEPARATED, HE GOT A HOLD OF JULIE... PULLED HER INTO A BACK ROOM. SEEMS HE'D BEEN LIVING IN THE PLACE... WE HAD NO IDEA ANYONE WAS EVEN THERE.
THIS SWEET OLD MAN... THE FIRST THING HE THINKS OF WHEN HE FINALLY SEES OTHER PEOPLE... HE TRIED TO RAPE JULIE. HAD I BEEN TWO MINUTES LATER WHEN I FOUND THEM... HE'D HAVE DONE IT.
I KILLED THAT MAN, RICK. I WANTED TO... BUT I DIDN'T MEAN TO. I BEAT ON HIM... AND HE DIED.

JESUS, MAN... DON'T BEAT YOURSELF UP OVER THAT... YOU DID WHAT *ANY* FATHER WOULD HAVE DONE IN THAT POSITION.

I MAY BE A COP... BUT I DON'T LET RULES *BLIND* ME TO WHAT'S RIGHT AND WRONG. *ESPECIALLY* IN LIGHT OF OUR CURRENT SITUATION.

I'M NOT BEATING MYSELF UP BECAUSE I *DID* IT... I'M BEATING MYSELF UP BECAUSE I DON'T FEEL *BAD* ABOUT DOING IT.

OH, SHIT.

ROAMERS.

ROAMERS?

YEAH-- THE END OF THE WORLD CHANGED *HIM*... BUT LOOK AT HOW IT CHANGED *ME.*

OH... YEAH, UM. WHEN WE WERE CAMPED NEAR ATLANTA, WE WENT INTO THE CITY... MOST OF THE ZOMBIES JUST SAT AROUND, NOT DOING ANYTHING UNLESS *PROVOKED.* IT SEEMED MOST OF THEM WERE CONTENT TO SIT AND DO *NOTHING* UNLESS SOMETHING HAPPENS BY THEM.

THEN OUR CAMP WAS *ATTACKED*... A PACK OF THOSE THINGS JUST TORE THROUGH US, KILLED TWO OF OUR FRIENDS. SO I GOTTA THINK THAT THERE ARE OTHER KINDS OF ZOMBIES THAT ROAM AROUND, ALWAYS ON THE MOVE.

I FIGURE *ROAMERS* IS AS GOOD A NAME AS ANY.

THEY'RE COMING THIS WAY... WE GOTTA DO SOMETHING.

WE'VE GOT AN *AXE* IN THE RV IF YOU WANT TO GRAB IT. GUNS MIGHT ATTRACT *MORE* OF THEM.

THIS *HAMMER* HAS WORKED JUST *FINE* FOR ME SO FAR.

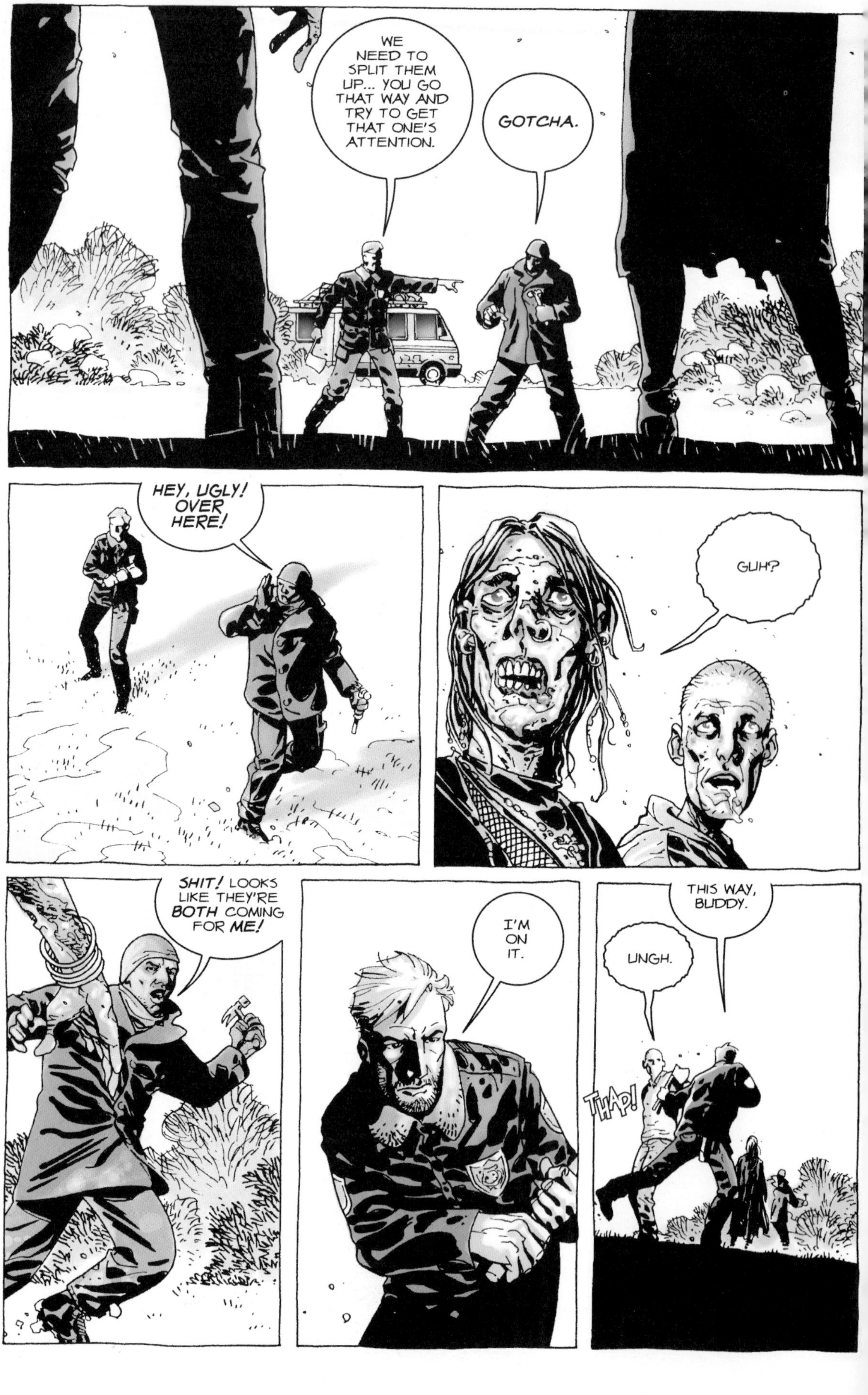
WE NEED TO SPLIT THEM UP... YOU GO THAT WAY AND TRY TO GET THAT ONE'S ATTENTION.
GOTCHA.
HEY, UGLY! OVER HERE!
GUH?
SHIT! LOOKS LIKE THEY'RE BOTH COMING FOR ME!
I'M ON IT.
THIS WAY, BUDDY.
UNGH.
THAP!

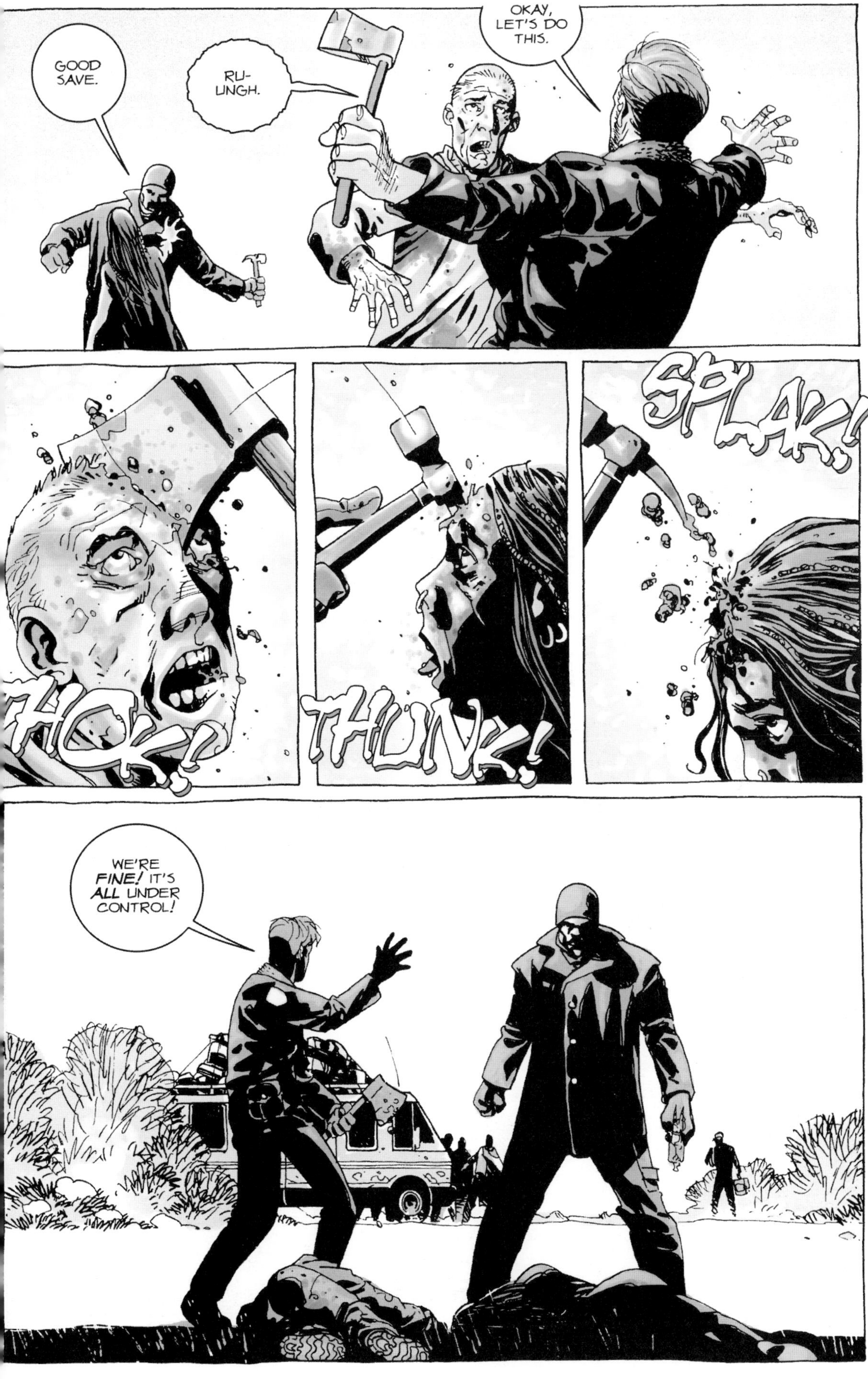
GOOD SAVE.
RU-UNGH.
OKAY, LET'S DO THIS.
HCK!
THUNK!
SPLAK!
WE'RE **FINE!** IT'S **ALL** UNDER CONTROL!

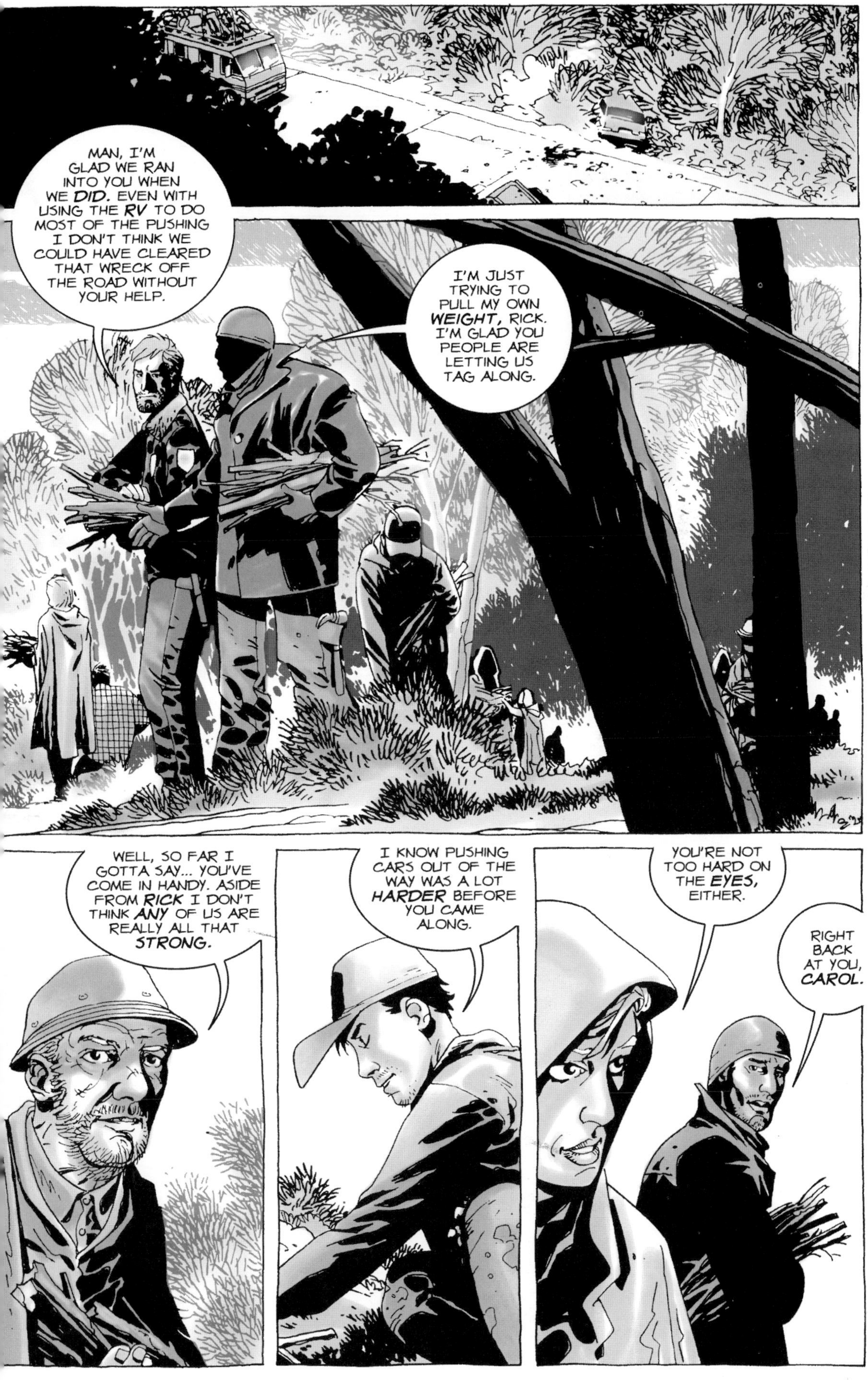
MAN, I'M GLAD WE RAN INTO YOU WHEN WE DID. EVEN WITH USING THE RV TO DO MOST OF THE PUSHING I DON'T THINK WE COULD HAVE CLEARED THAT WRECK OFF THE ROAD WITHOUT YOUR HELP.
I'M JUST TRYING TO PULL MY OWN WEIGHT, RICK. I'M GLAD YOU PEOPLE ARE LETTING US TAG ALONG.
WELL, SO FAR I GOTTA SAY... YOU'VE COME IN HANDY. ASIDE FROM RICK I DON'T THINK ANY OF US ARE REALLY ALL THAT STRONG.
I KNOW PUSHING CARS OUT OF THE WAY WAS A LOT HARDER BEFORE YOU CAME ALONG.
YOU'RE NOT TOO HARD ON THE EYES, EITHER.
RIGHT BACK AT YOU, CAROL.

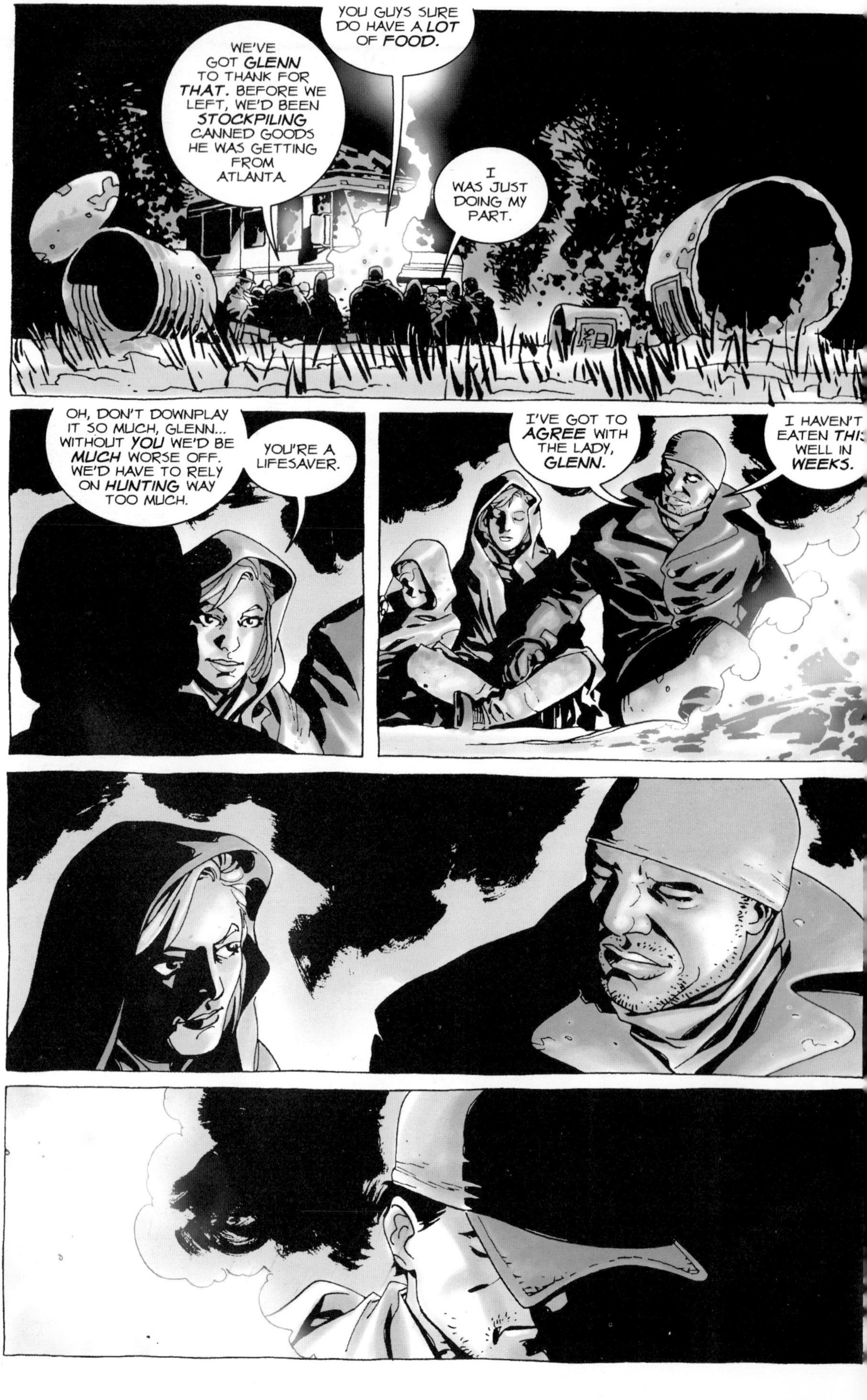
YOU GUYS SURE DO HAVE A LOT OF FOOD.
WE'VE GOT GLENN TO THANK FOR THAT. BEFORE WE LEFT, WE'D BEEN STOCKPILING CANNED GOODS HE WAS GETTING FROM ATLANTA.
I WAS JUST DOING MY PART.
OH, DON'T DOWNPLAY IT SO MUCH, GLENN... WITHOUT YOU WE'D BE MUCH WORSE OFF. WE'D HAVE TO RELY ON HUNTING WAY TOO MUCH.
YOU'RE A LIFESAVER.
I'VE GOT TO AGREE WITH THE LADY, GLENN.
I HAVEN'T EATEN THIS WELL IN WEEKS.

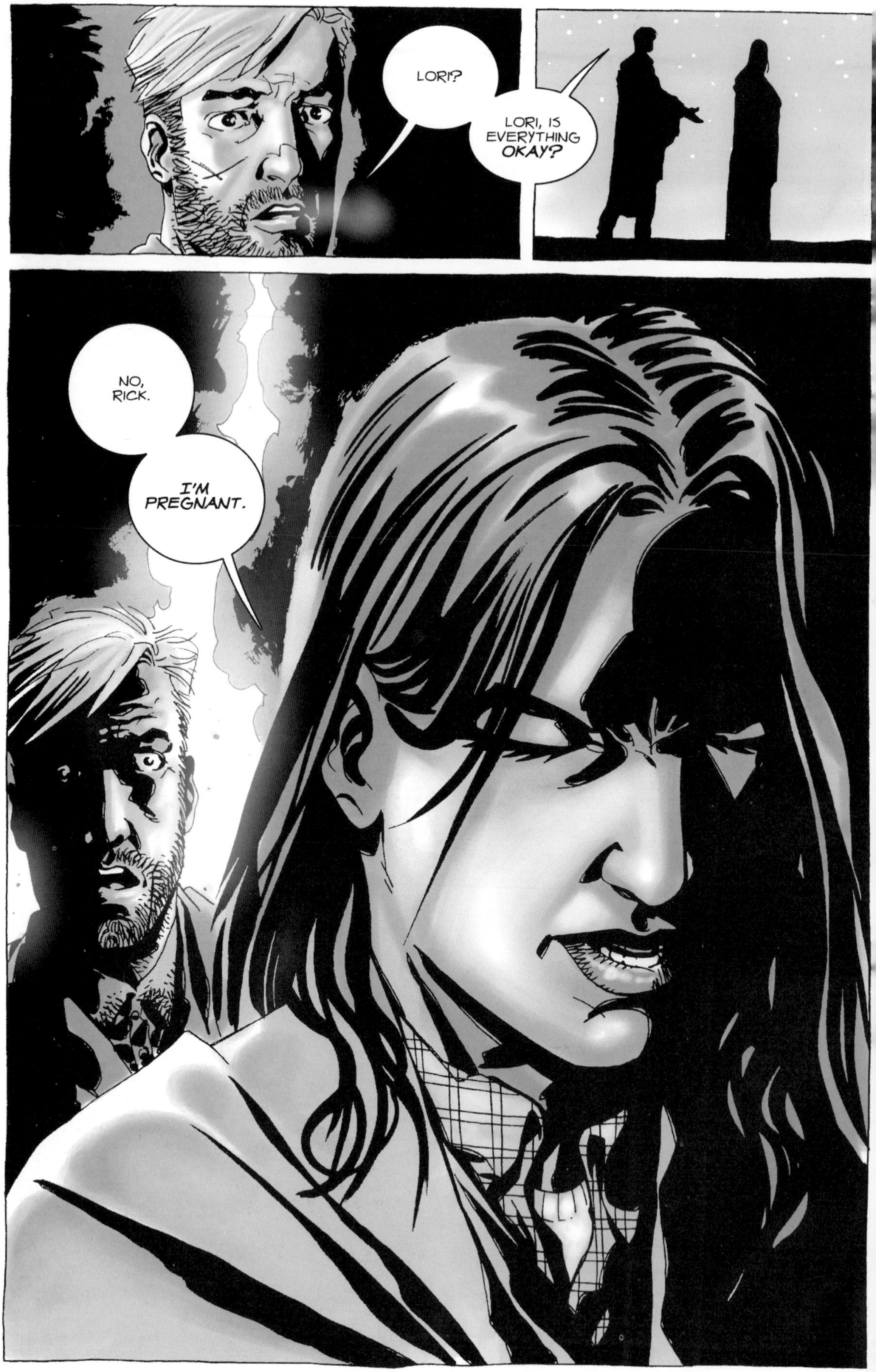
LORI?
LORI, IS EVERYTHING OKAY?
NO, RICK.
I'M PREGNANT.

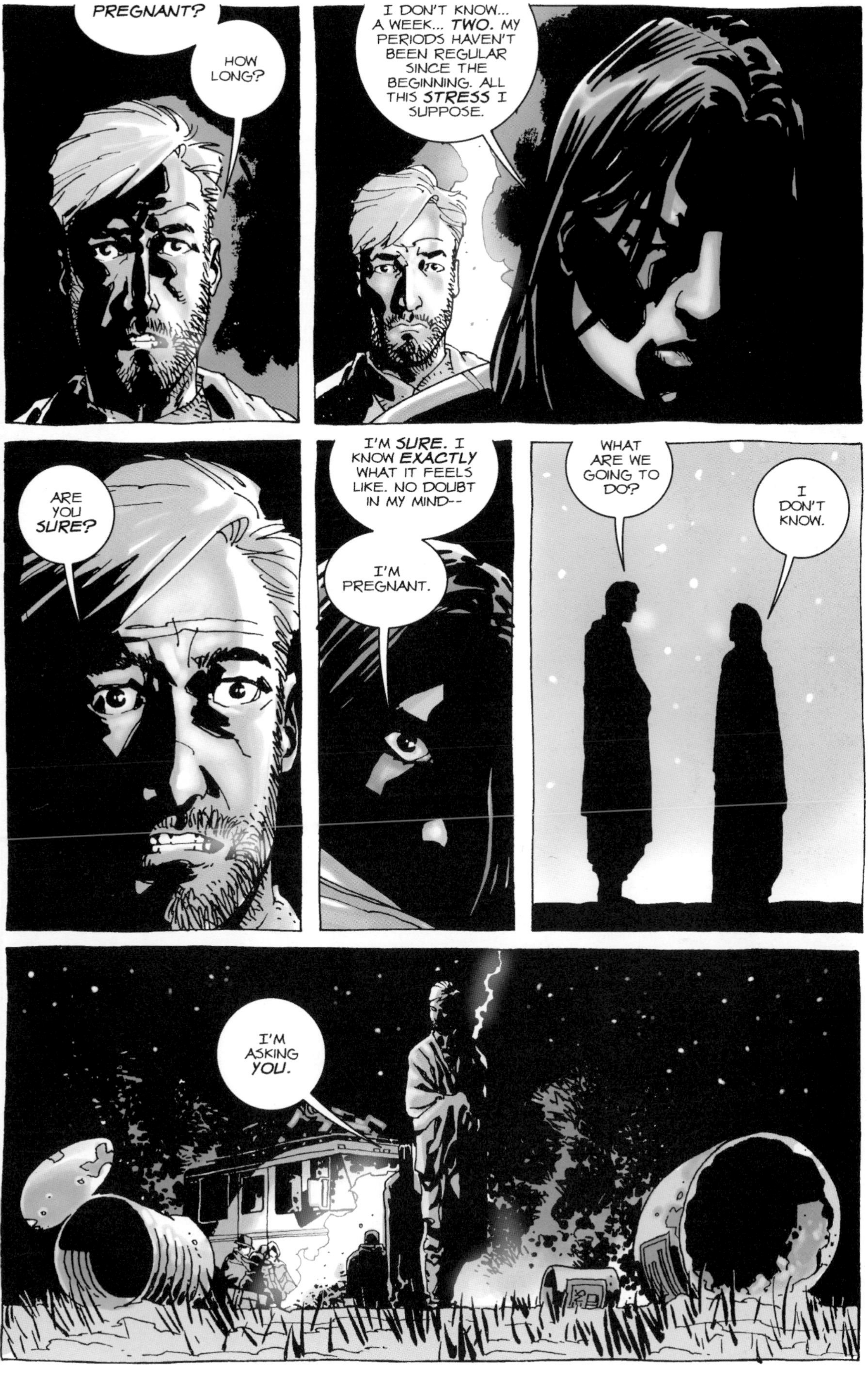
PREGNANT?
HOW LONG?
I DON'T KNOW... A WEEK... TWO. MY PERIODS HAVEN'T BEEN REGULAR SINCE THE BEGINNING. ALL THIS STRESS I SUPPOSE.
ARE YOU SURE?
I'M SURE. I KNOW EXACTLY WHAT IT FEELS LIKE. NO DOUBT IN MY MIND--
I'M PREGNANT.
WHAT ARE WE GOING TO DO?
I DON'T KNOW.
I'M ASKING YOU.

EVERYTHING OKAY?

I'M PREGNANT.

I JUST WANTED TO TELL *RICK* FIRST.

WE'RE GOING TO HAVE A BABY.

UM... *WOW.* I JUST--I DON'T KNOW WHAT TO *SAY.*

"CONGRATULATIONS" HAS WORKED FOR *YEARS.*

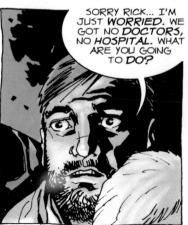

SORRY RICK... I'M JUST *WORRIED.* WE GOT NO *DOCTORS,* NO *HOSPITAL.* WHAT ARE YOU GOING TO *DO?*

WE'LL CROSS THAT BRIDGE WHEN WE COME TO IT.

WE'RE GOING TO BE *FINE,* ALLEN. THIS IS *GOOD* NEWS.

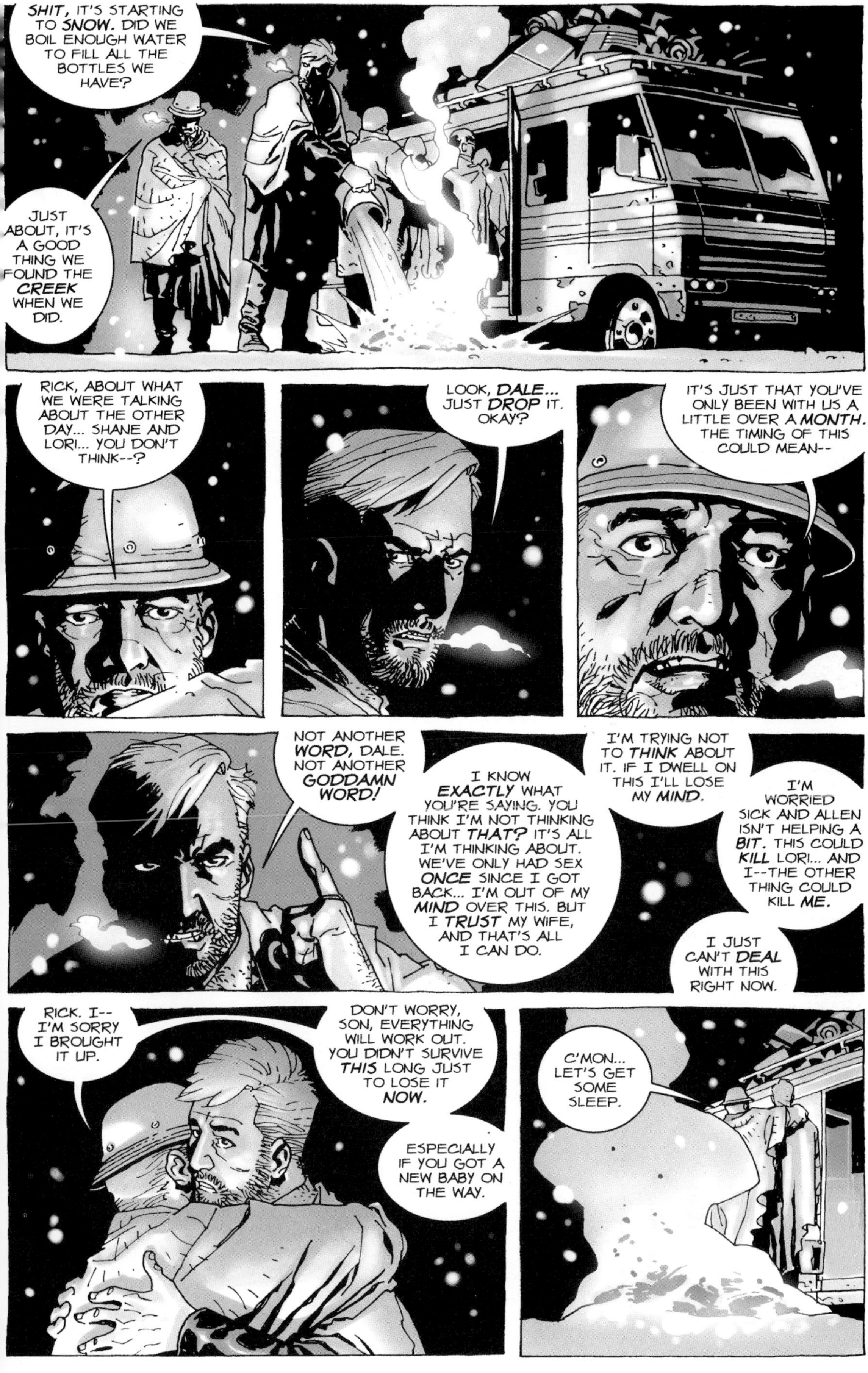
SHIT, IT'S STARTING TO SNOW. DID WE BOIL ENOUGH WATER TO FILL ALL THE BOTTLES WE HAVE?
JUST ABOUT, IT'S A GOOD THING WE FOUND THE CREEK WHEN WE DID.
RICK, ABOUT WHAT WE WERE TALKING ABOUT THE OTHER DAY... SHANE AND LORI... YOU DON'T THINK--?
LOOK, DALE... JUST DROP IT. OKAY?
IT'S JUST THAT YOU'VE ONLY BEEN WITH US A LITTLE OVER A MONTH. THE TIMING OF THIS COULD MEAN--
NOT ANOTHER WORD, DALE. NOT ANOTHER GODDAMN WORD!
I KNOW EXACTLY WHAT YOU'RE SAYING. YOU THINK I'M NOT THINKING ABOUT THAT? IT'S ALL I'M THINKING ABOUT. WE'VE ONLY HAD SEX ONCE SINCE I GOT BACK... I'M OUT OF MY MIND OVER THIS. BUT I TRUST MY WIFE, AND THAT'S ALL I CAN DO.
I'M TRYING NOT TO THINK ABOUT IT. IF I DWELL ON THIS I'LL LOSE MY MIND.
I'M WORRIED SICK AND ALLEN ISN'T HELPING A BIT. THIS COULD KILL LORI... AND I--THE OTHER THING COULD KILL ME.
I JUST CAN'T DEAL WITH THIS RIGHT NOW.
RICK. I-- I'M SORRY I BROUGHT IT UP.
DON'T WORRY, SON, EVERYTHING WILL WORK OUT. YOU DIDN'T SURVIVE THIS LONG JUST TO LOSE IT NOW.
ESPECIALLY IF YOU GOT A NEW BABY ON THE WAY.
C'MON... LET'S GET SOME SLEEP.

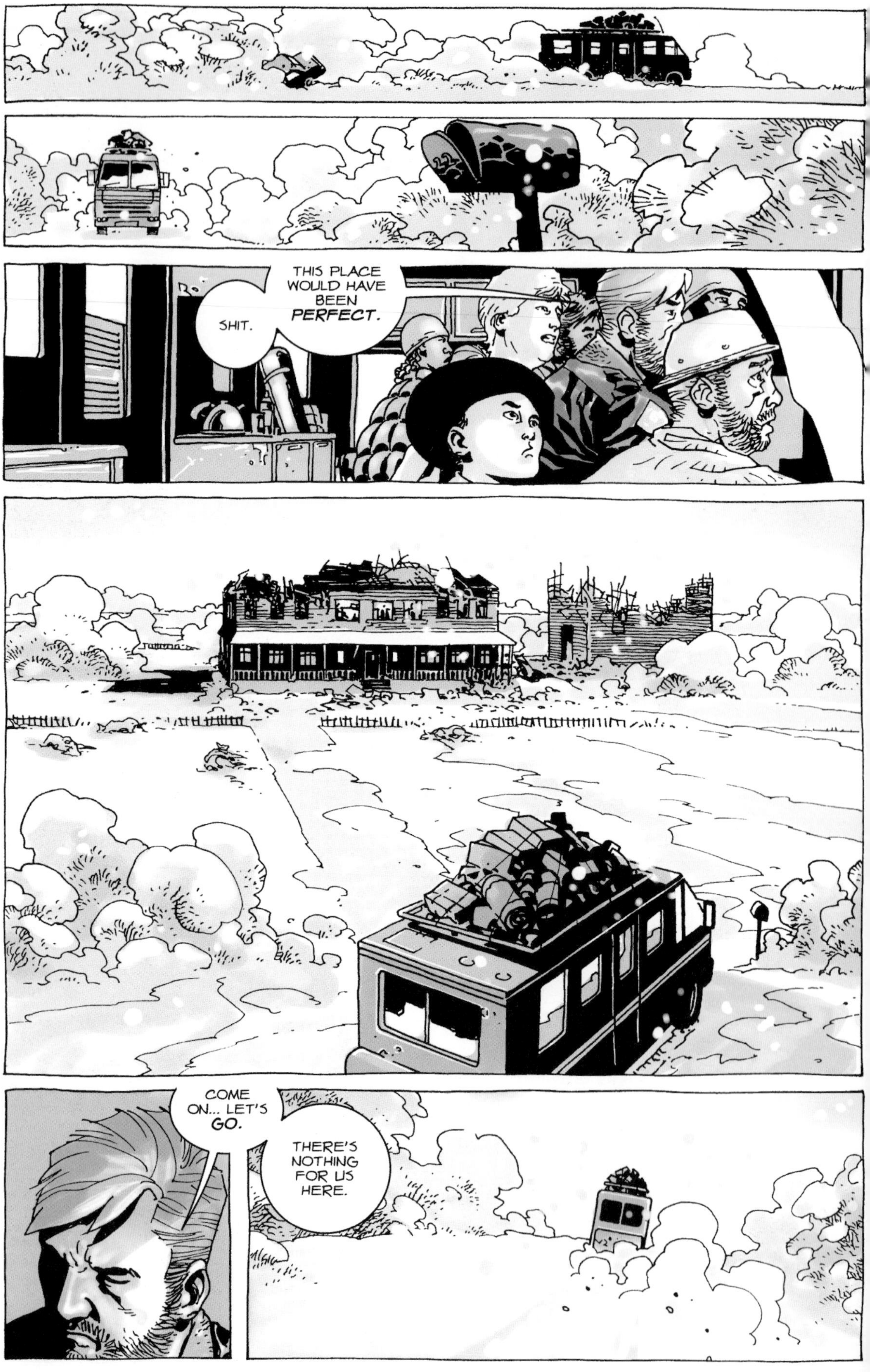
SHIT.
THIS PLACE WOULD HAVE BEEN PERFECT.
COME ON... LET'S GO.
THERE'S NOTHING FOR US HERE.

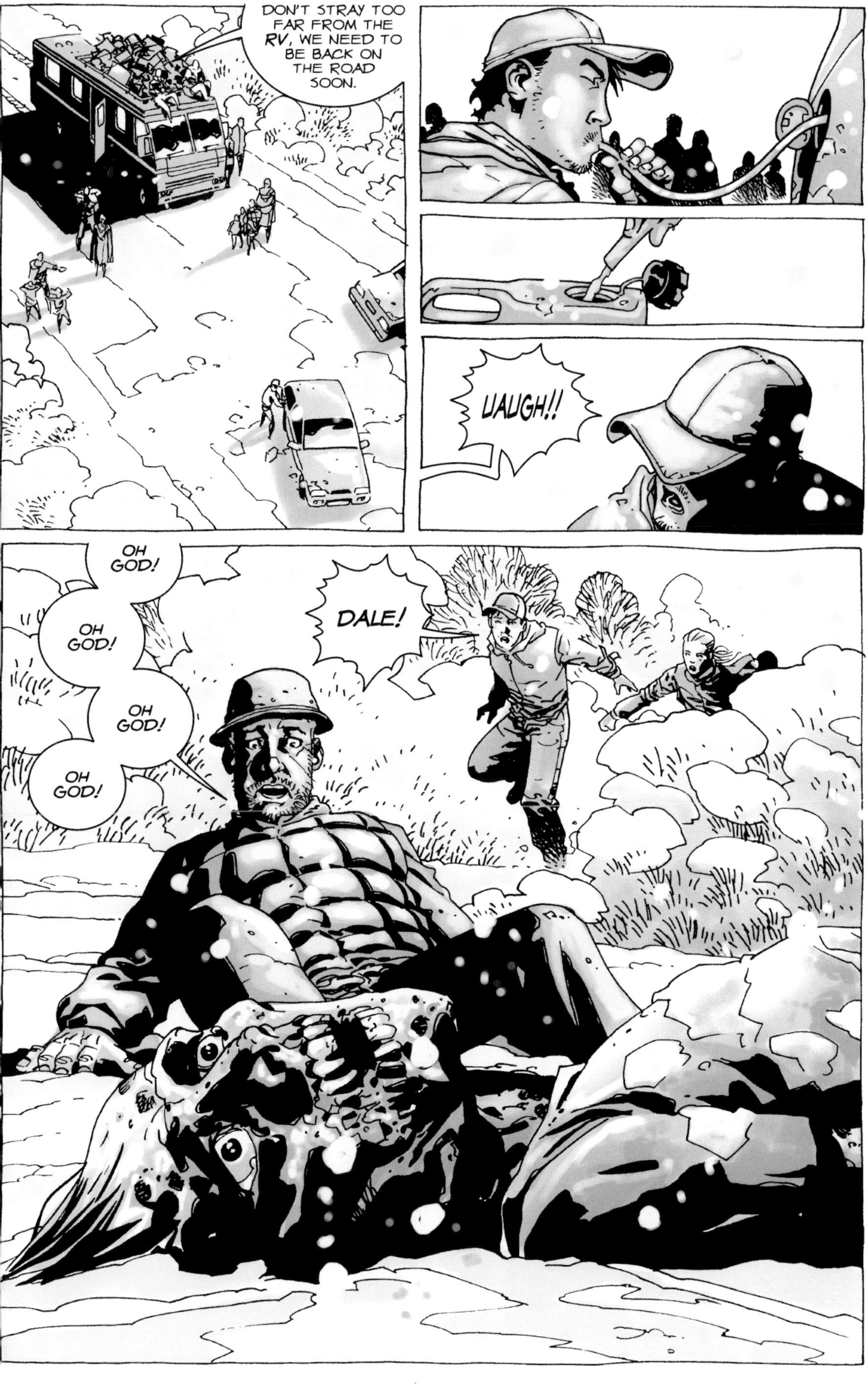
DON'T STRAY TOO FAR FROM THE RV, WE NEED TO BE BACK ON THE ROAD SOON.
UAUGH!!
OH GOD!
OH GOD!
OH GOD!
OH GOD!
DALE!

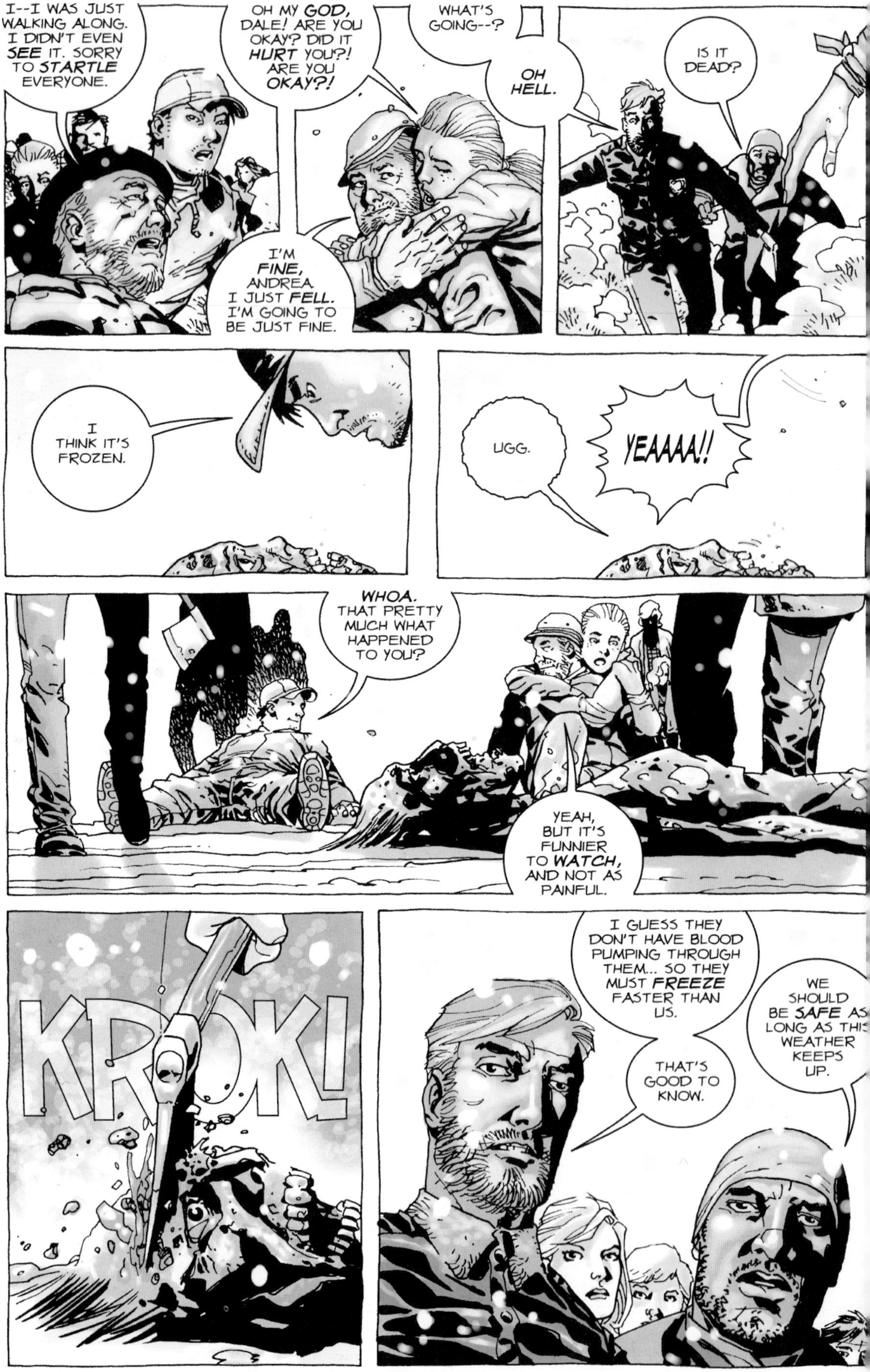
I--I WAS JUST WALKING ALONG. I DIDN'T EVEN SEE IT. SORRY TO STARTLE EVERYONE.
OH MY GOD, DALE! ARE YOU OKAY? DID IT HURT YOU?! ARE YOU OKAY?!
I'M FINE, ANDREA. I JUST FELL. I'M GOING TO BE JUST FINE.
WHAT'S GOING--?
OH HELL.
IS IT DEAD?
I THINK IT'S FROZEN.
UGG.
YEAAAA!!
WHOA. THAT PRETTY MUCH WHAT HAPPENED TO YOU?
YEAH, BUT IT'S FUNNIER TO WATCH, AND NOT AS PAINFUL.
KROK!
I GUESS THEY DON'T HAVE BLOOD PUMPING THROUGH THEM... SO THEY MUST FREEZE FASTER THAN US.
THAT'S GOOD TO KNOW.
WE SHOULD BE SAFE AS LONG AS THIS WEATHER KEEPS UP.

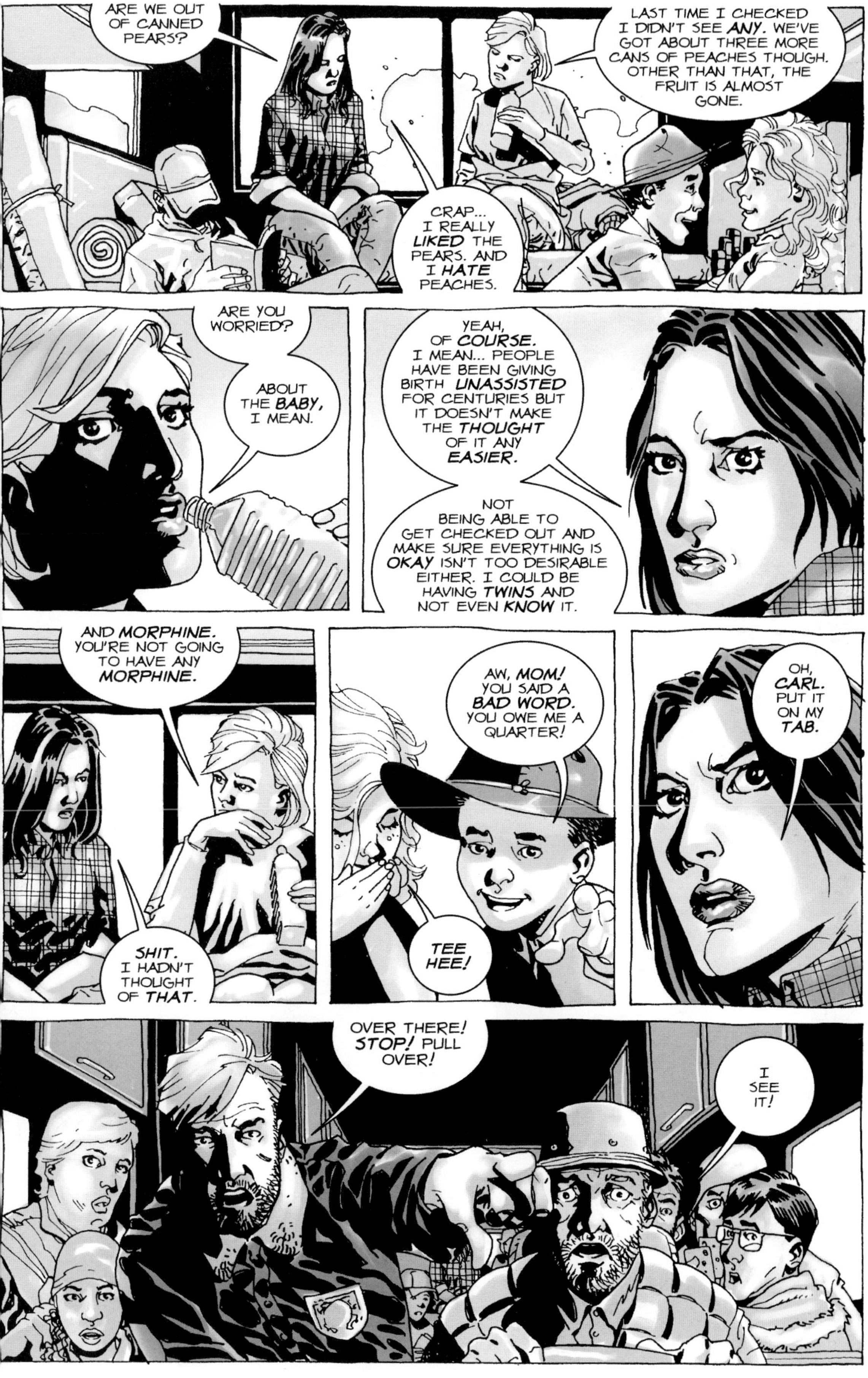
ARE WE OUT OF CANNED PEARS?
LAST TIME I CHECKED I DIDN'T SEE ANY. WE'VE GOT ABOUT THREE MORE CANS OF PEACHES THOUGH. OTHER THAN THAT, THE FRUIT IS ALMOST GONE.
CRAP... I REALLY LIKED THE PEARS. AND I HATE PEACHES.
ARE YOU WORRIED?
ABOUT THE BABY, I MEAN.
YEAH, OF COURSE. I MEAN... PEOPLE HAVE BEEN GIVING BIRTH UNASSISTED FOR CENTURIES BUT IT DOESN'T MAKE THE THOUGHT OF IT ANY EASIER.
NOT BEING ABLE TO GET CHECKED OUT AND MAKE SURE EVERYTHING IS OKAY ISN'T TOO DESIRABLE EITHER. I COULD BE HAVING TWINS AND NOT EVEN KNOW IT.
AND MORPHINE. YOU'RE NOT GOING TO HAVE ANY MORPHINE.
SHIT. I HADN'T THOUGHT OF THAT.
AW, MOM! YOU SAID A BAD WORD. YOU OWE ME A QUARTER!
TEE HEE!
OH, CARL. PUT IT ON MY TAB.
OVER THERE! STOP! PULL OVER!
I SEE IT!

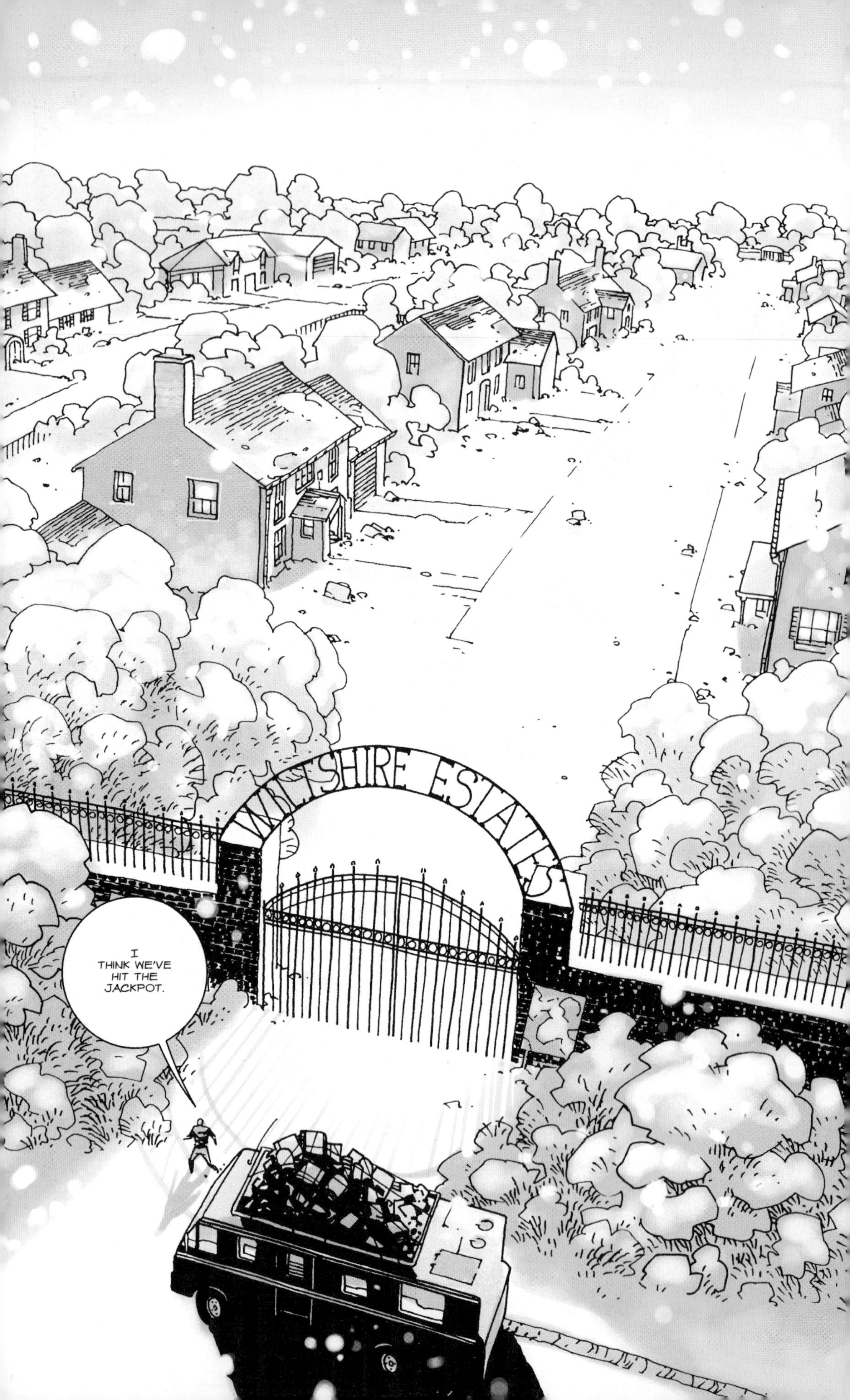
I THINK WE'VE HIT THE JACKPOT.

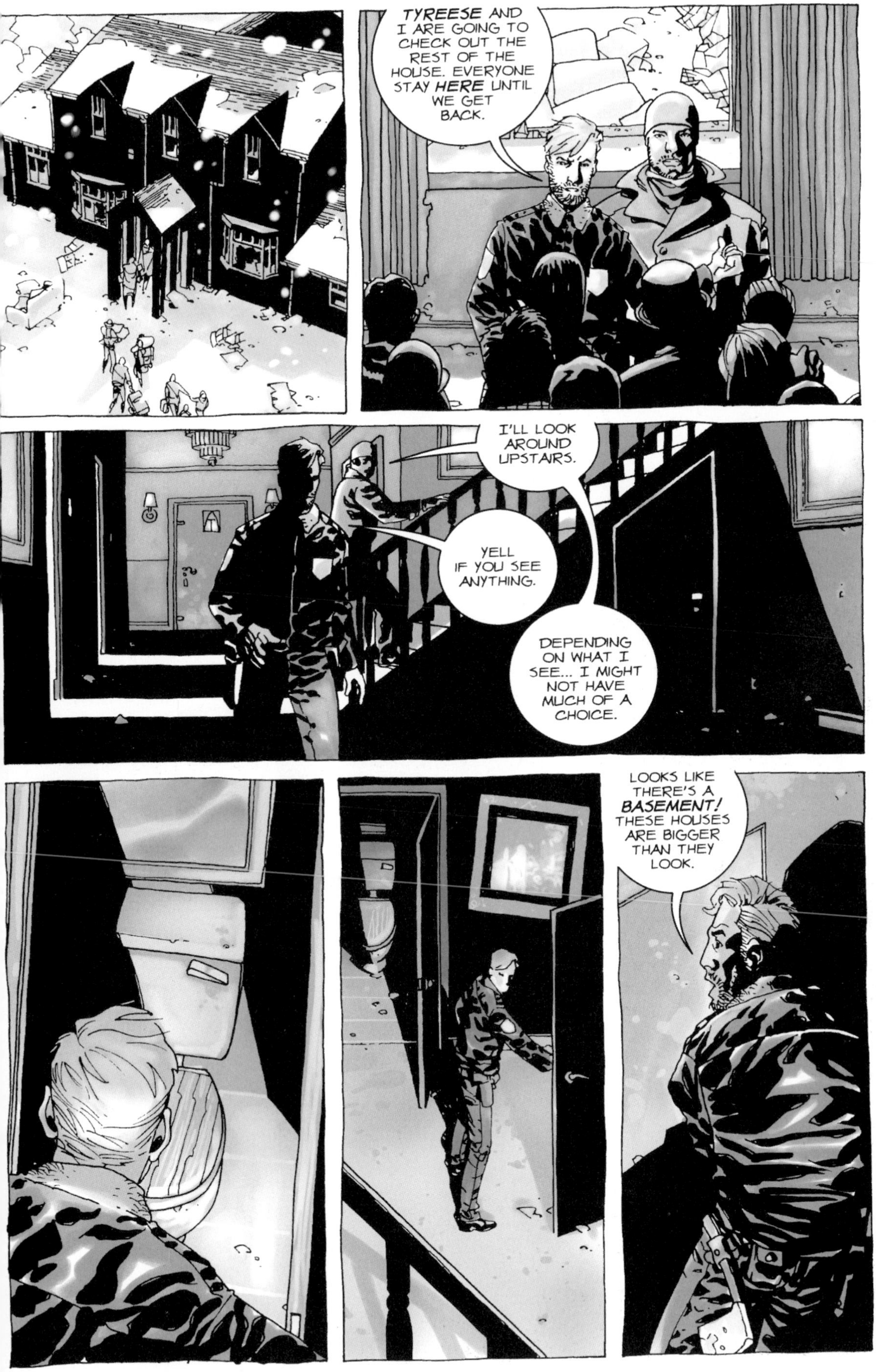
TYREESE AND I ARE GOING TO CHECK OUT THE REST OF THE HOUSE. EVERYONE STAY HERE UNTIL WE GET BACK.
I'LL LOOK AROUND UPSTAIRS.
YELL IF YOU SEE ANYTHING.
DEPENDING ON WHAT I SEE... I MIGHT NOT HAVE MUCH OF A CHOICE.
LOOKS LIKE THERE'S A BASEMENT! THESE HOUSES ARE BIGGER THAN THEY LOOK.

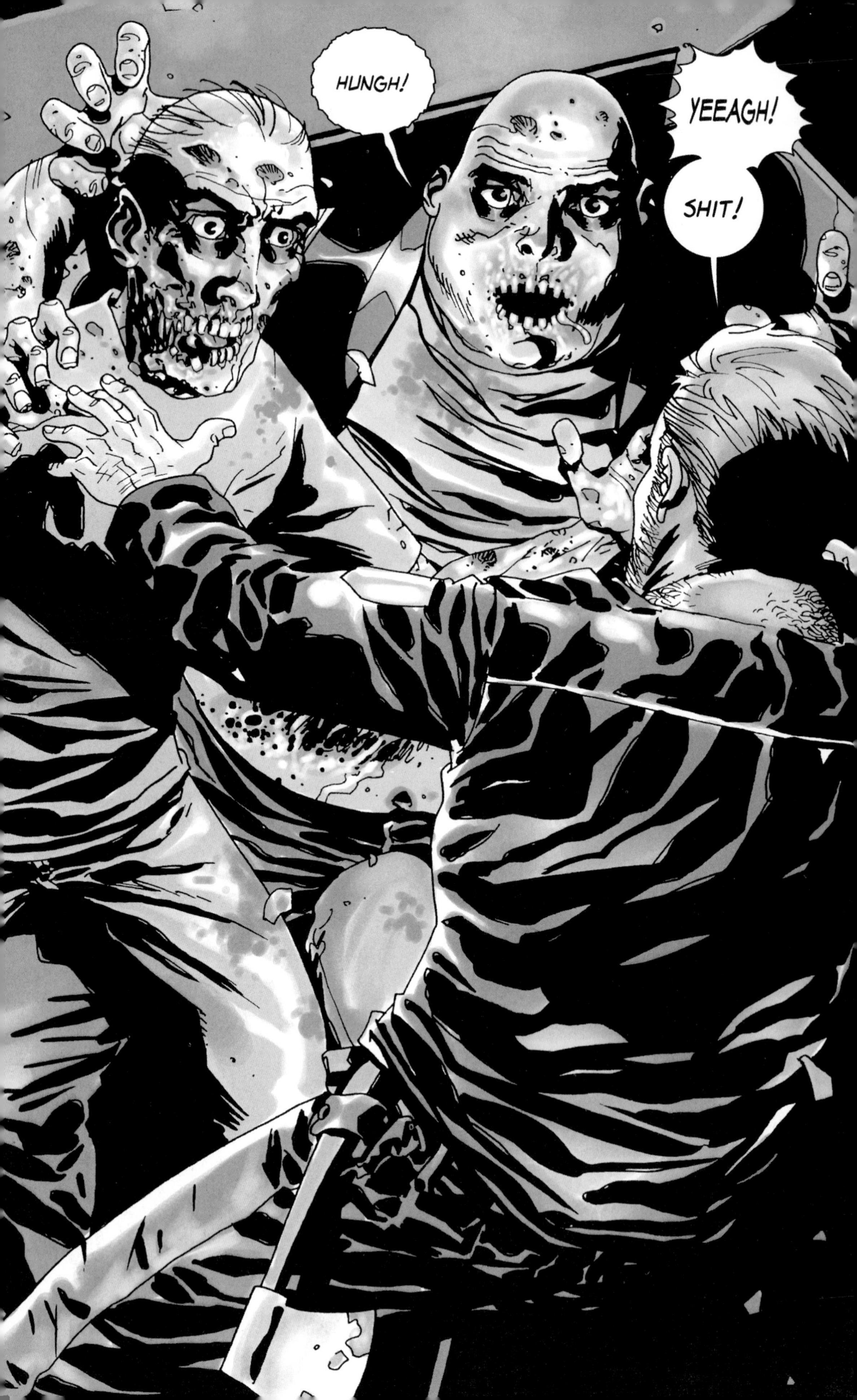
HUNGH!
YEEAGH!
SHIT!

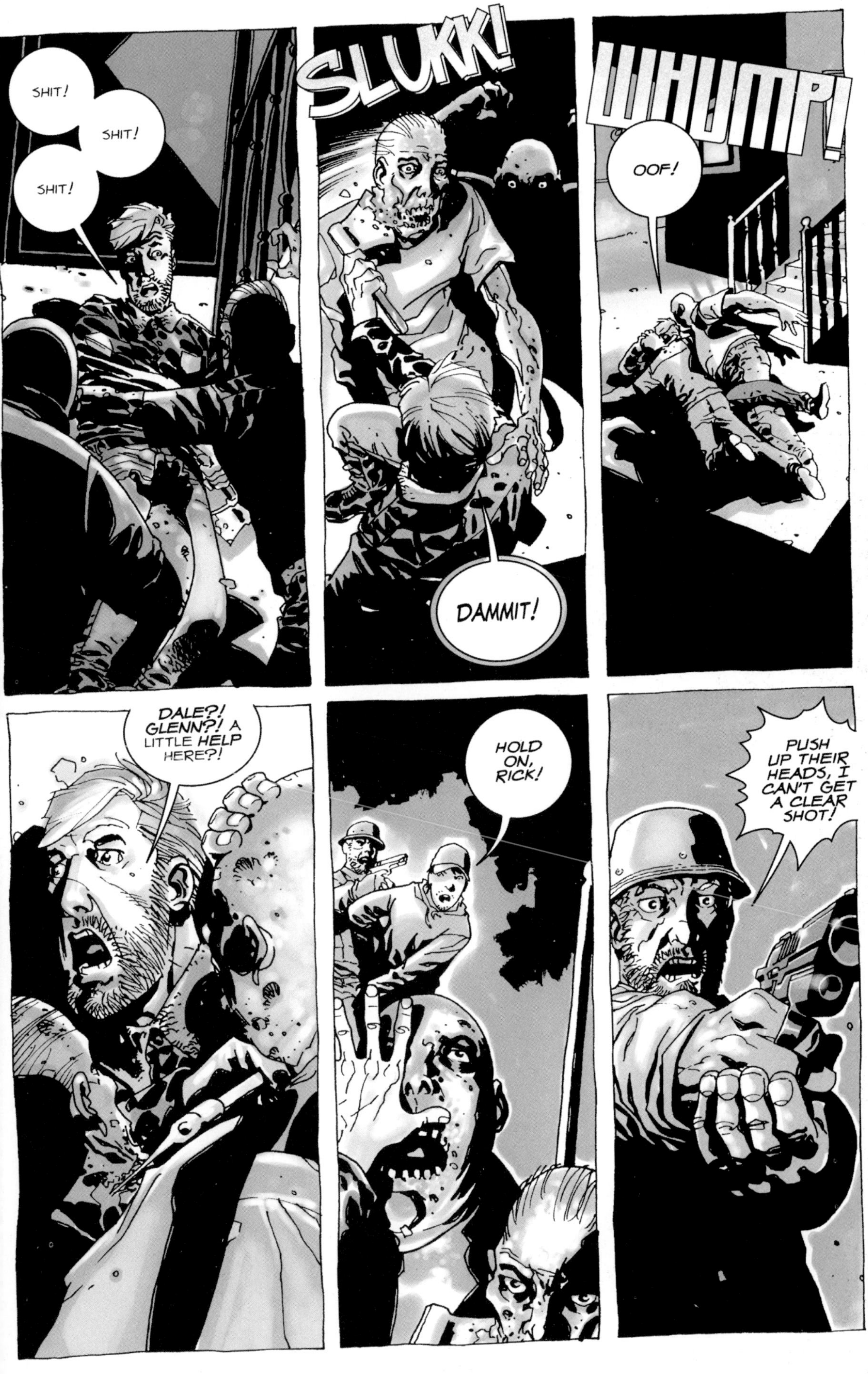
SHIT!
SHIT!
SHIT!
SLUKK!
DAMMIT!
WHUMP!
OOF!
DALE?! GLENN?! A LITTLE HELP HERE?!
HOLD ON, RICK!
PUSH UP THEIR HEADS, I CAN'T GET A CLEAR SHOT!

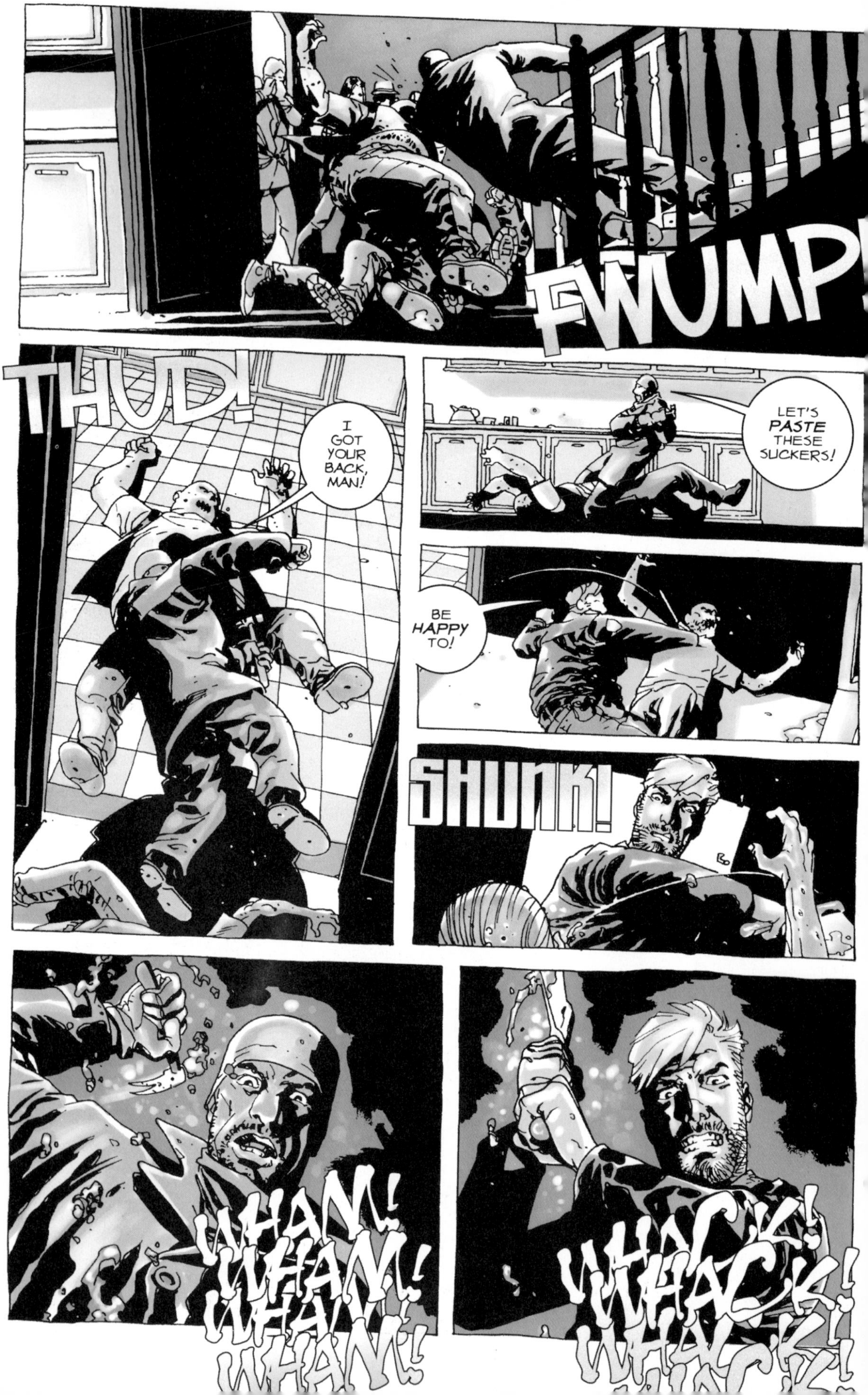
FWUMP!
THUD!
I GOT YOUR BACK, MAN!
LET'S PASTE THESE SUCKERS!
BE HAPPY TO!
SHUNK!
WHAM! WHAM! WHAM! WHAM!
WHACK! WHACK! WHACK!

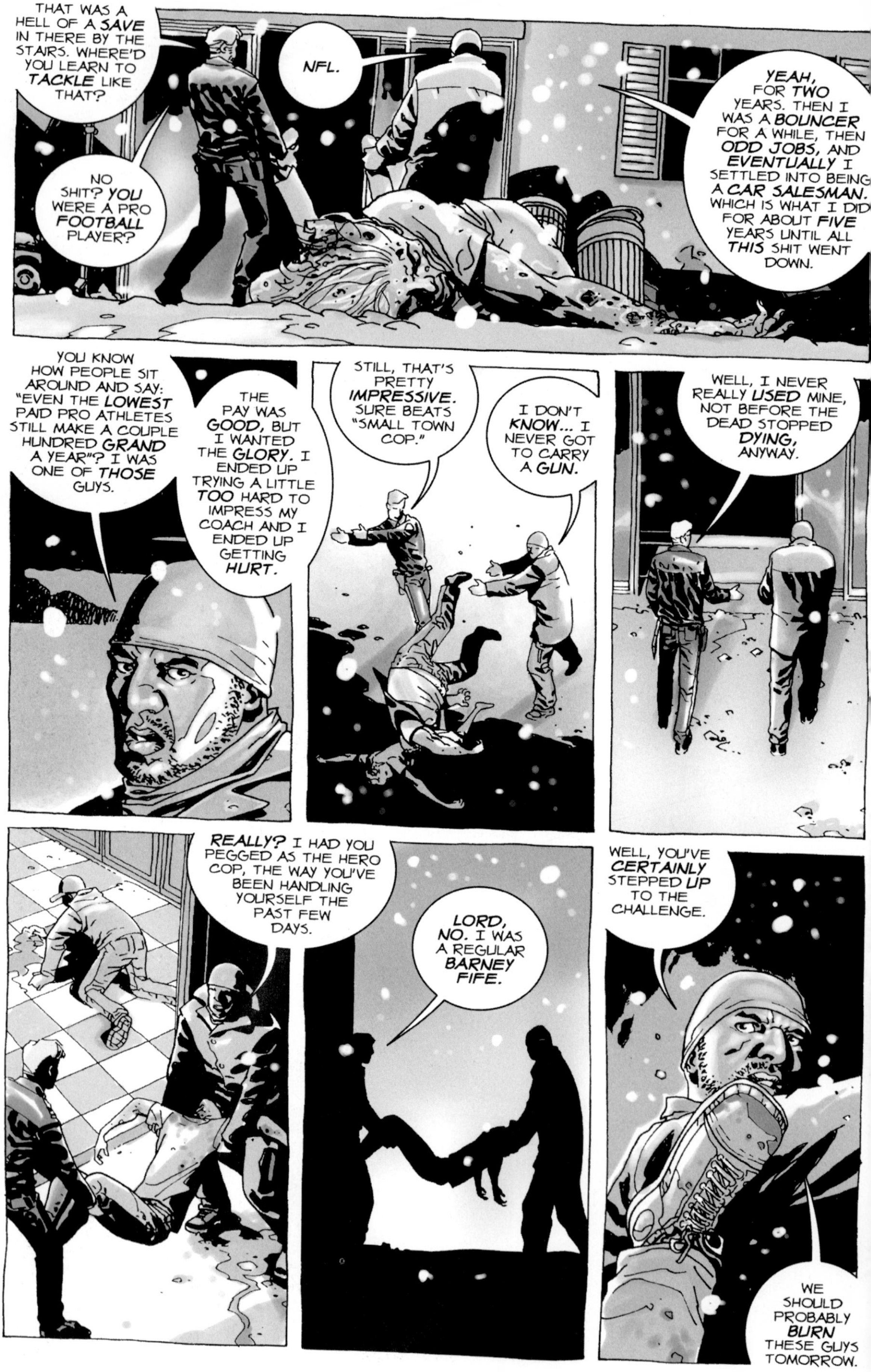
THAT WAS A HELL OF A SAVE IN THERE BY THE STAIRS. WHERE'D YOU LEARN TO TACKLE LIKE THAT?
NFL.
NO SHIT? YOU WERE A PRO FOOTBALL PLAYER?
YEAH, FOR TWO YEARS. THEN I WAS A BOUNCER FOR A WHILE, THEN ODD JOBS, AND EVENTUALLY I SETTLED INTO BEING A CAR SALESMAN. WHICH IS WHAT I DID FOR ABOUT FIVE YEARS UNTIL ALL THIS SHIT WENT DOWN.
YOU KNOW HOW PEOPLE SIT AROUND AND SAY: "EVEN THE LOWEST PAID PRO ATHLETES STILL MAKE A COUPLE HUNDRED GRAND A YEAR"? I WAS ONE OF THOSE GUYS.
THE PAY WAS GOOD, BUT I WANTED THE GLORY. I ENDED UP TRYING A LITTLE TOO HARD TO IMPRESS MY COACH AND I ENDED UP GETTING HURT.
STILL, THAT'S PRETTY IMPRESSIVE. SURE BEATS "SMALL TOWN COP."
I DON'T KNOW... I NEVER GOT TO CARRY A GUN.
WELL, I NEVER REALLY USED MINE, NOT BEFORE THE DEAD STOPPED DYING, ANYWAY.
REALLY? I HAD YOU PEGGED AS THE HERO COP, THE WAY YOU'VE BEEN HANDLING YOURSELF THE PAST FEW DAYS.
LORD, NO. I WAS A REGULAR BARNEY FIFE.
WELL, YOU'VE CERTAINLY STEPPED UP TO THE CHALLENGE.
WE SHOULD PROBABLY BURN THESE GUYS TOMORROW.

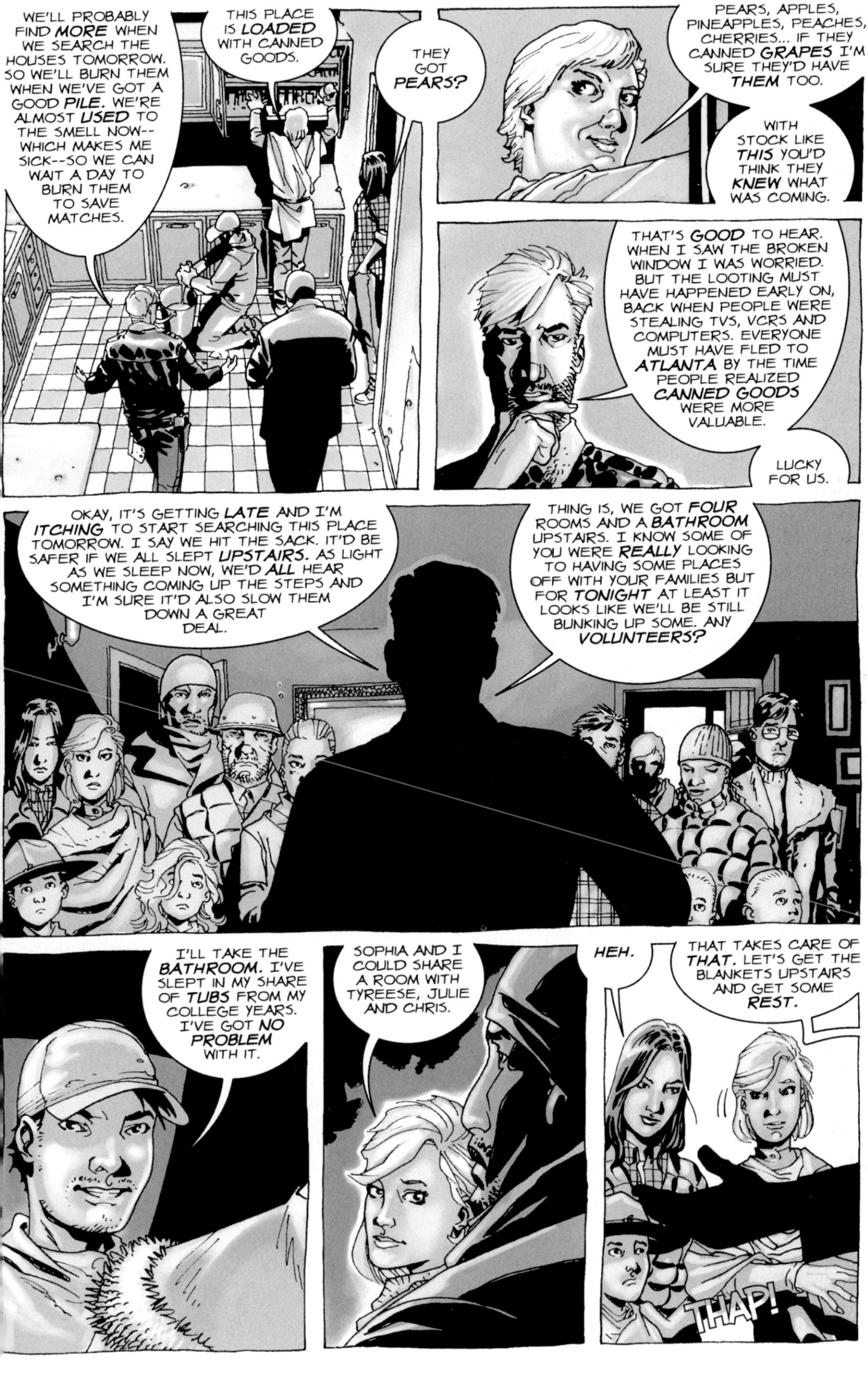
WE'LL PROBABLY FIND MORE WHEN WE SEARCH THE HOUSES TOMORROW. SO WE'LL BURN THEM WHEN WE'VE GOT A GOOD PILE. WE'RE ALMOST USED TO THE SMELL NOW-- WHICH MAKES ME SICK--SO WE CAN WAIT A DAY TO BURN THEM TO SAVE MATCHES.
THIS PLACE IS LOADED WITH CANNED GOODS.
THEY GOT PEARS?
PEARS, APPLES, PINEAPPLES, PEACHES, CHERRIES... IF THEY CANNED GRAPES I'M SURE THEY'D HAVE THEM TOO.
WITH STOCK LIKE THIS YOU'D THINK THEY KNEW WHAT WAS COMING.
THAT'S GOOD TO HEAR. WHEN I SAW THE BROKEN WINDOW I WAS WORRIED. BUT THE LOOTING MUST HAVE HAPPENED EARLY ON, BACK WHEN PEOPLE WERE STEALING TVS, VCRS AND COMPUTERS. EVERYONE MUST HAVE FLED TO ATLANTA BY THE TIME PEOPLE REALIZED CANNED GOODS WERE MORE VALUABLE.
LUCKY FOR US.
OKAY, IT'S GETTING LATE AND I'M ITCHING TO START SEARCHING THIS PLACE TOMORROW. I SAY WE HIT THE SACK. IT'D BE SAFER IF WE ALL SLEPT UPSTAIRS. AS LIGHT AS WE SLEEP NOW, WE'D ALL HEAR SOMETHING COMING UP THE STEPS AND I'M SURE IT'D ALSO SLOW THEM DOWN A GREAT DEAL.
THING IS, WE GOT FOUR ROOMS AND A BATHROOM UPSTAIRS. I KNOW SOME OF YOU WERE REALLY LOOKING TO HAVING SOME PLACES OFF WITH YOUR FAMILIES BUT FOR TONIGHT AT LEAST IT LOOKS LIKE WE'LL BE STILL BUNKING UP SOME. ANY VOLUNTEERS?
I'LL TAKE THE BATHROOM. I'VE SLEPT IN MY SHARE OF TUBS FROM MY COLLEGE YEARS. I'VE GOT NO PROBLEM WITH IT.
SOPHIA AND I COULD SHARE A ROOM WITH TYREESE, JULIE AND CHRIS.
HEH.
THAT TAKES CARE OF THAT. LET'S GET THE BLANKETS UPSTAIRS AND GET SOME REST.
THAP!

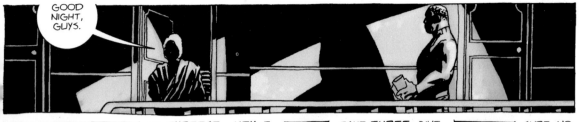

GOOD NIGHT, GUYS.

OH, *TYREESE...* HEY. I FOUND SOME *BLANKETS* IN OUR CLOSET. THERE'S ENOUGH FOR EVERYONE TO HAVE *ONE* EXTRA

TAKE *THREE.* GIVE ONE TO CAROL AND SOPHIA. AND CAN YOU SWING THE THIRD BY THE BATHROOM AND GIVE IT TO *GLENN?*

SURE. NO PROBLEM, DONNA AND THANKS.

HEY, TYREESE. I DON'T THINK I'VE GOTTEN A CHANCE TO WELCOME YOU TO OUR GROUP. I'M REALLY *GLAD* YOU'VE DECIDED TO STICK AROUND. YOU'VE REALLY BEEN A *BIG* HELP, AND JULIE IS THE *SWEETEST* LITTLE GIRL.

WELL THAT'S NICE OF YOU TO SAY. WE'RE REALLY *LUCKY* TO HAVE FOUND SUCH NICE PEOPLE. ESPECIALLY WHEN WE DID... WE WERE OUT OF *FOOD,* WITH NO *SHELTER...* WE PROBABLY WOULDN'T HAVE MADE IT IF WE HADN'T RAN INTO YOU THAT NIGHT.

I *REALLY* APPRECIATE ALL YOU PEOPLE HAVE GIVEN US. YOU CAN *ALWAYS* COUNT ON ME TO DO MY PART AROUND HERE.

GOODNIGHT, DONNA.

GOODNIGHT, *TYREESE.* SLEEP WELL.

DALE?

ANDREA?

GUYS, I FOUND--

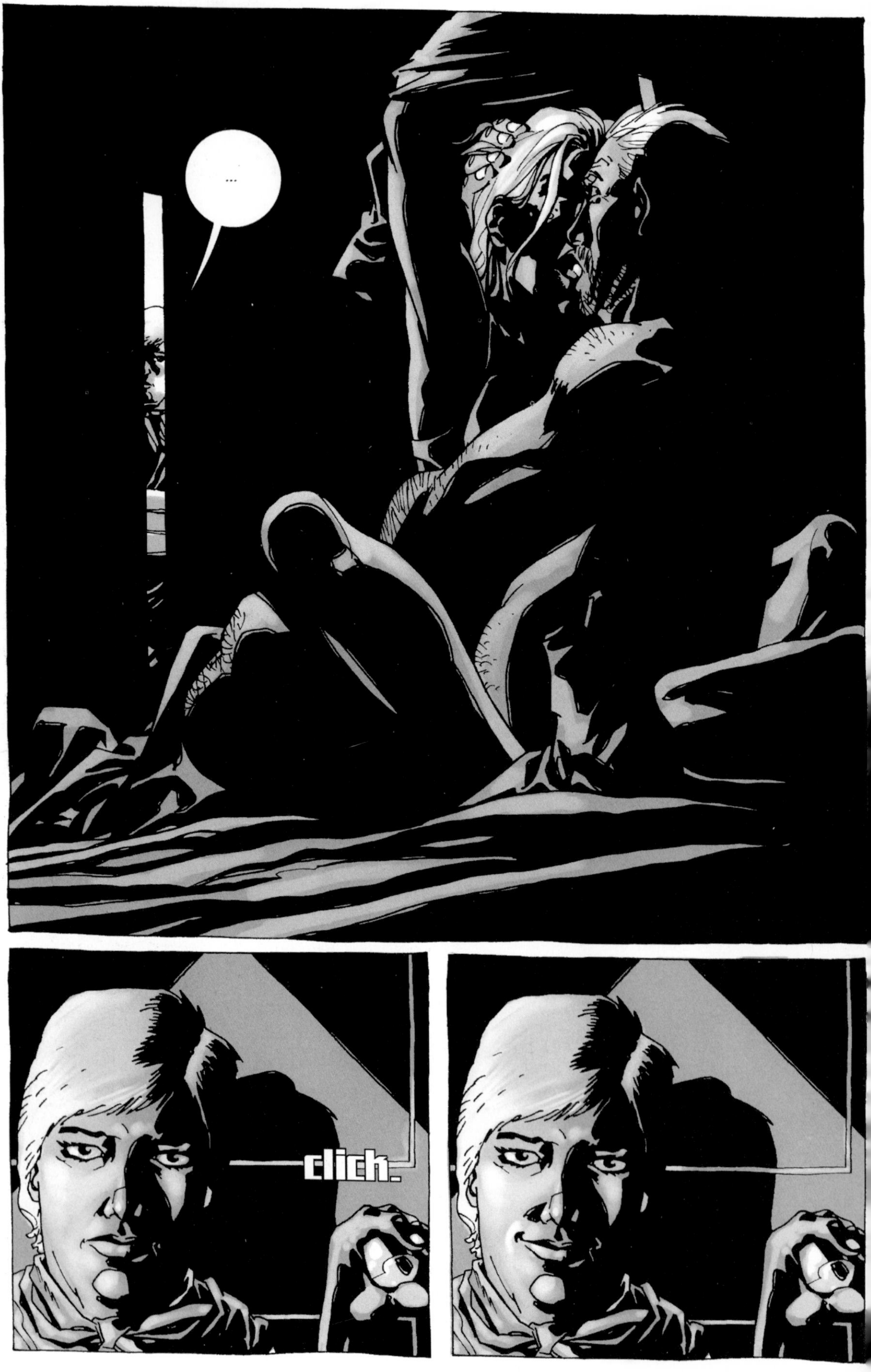
...
click.

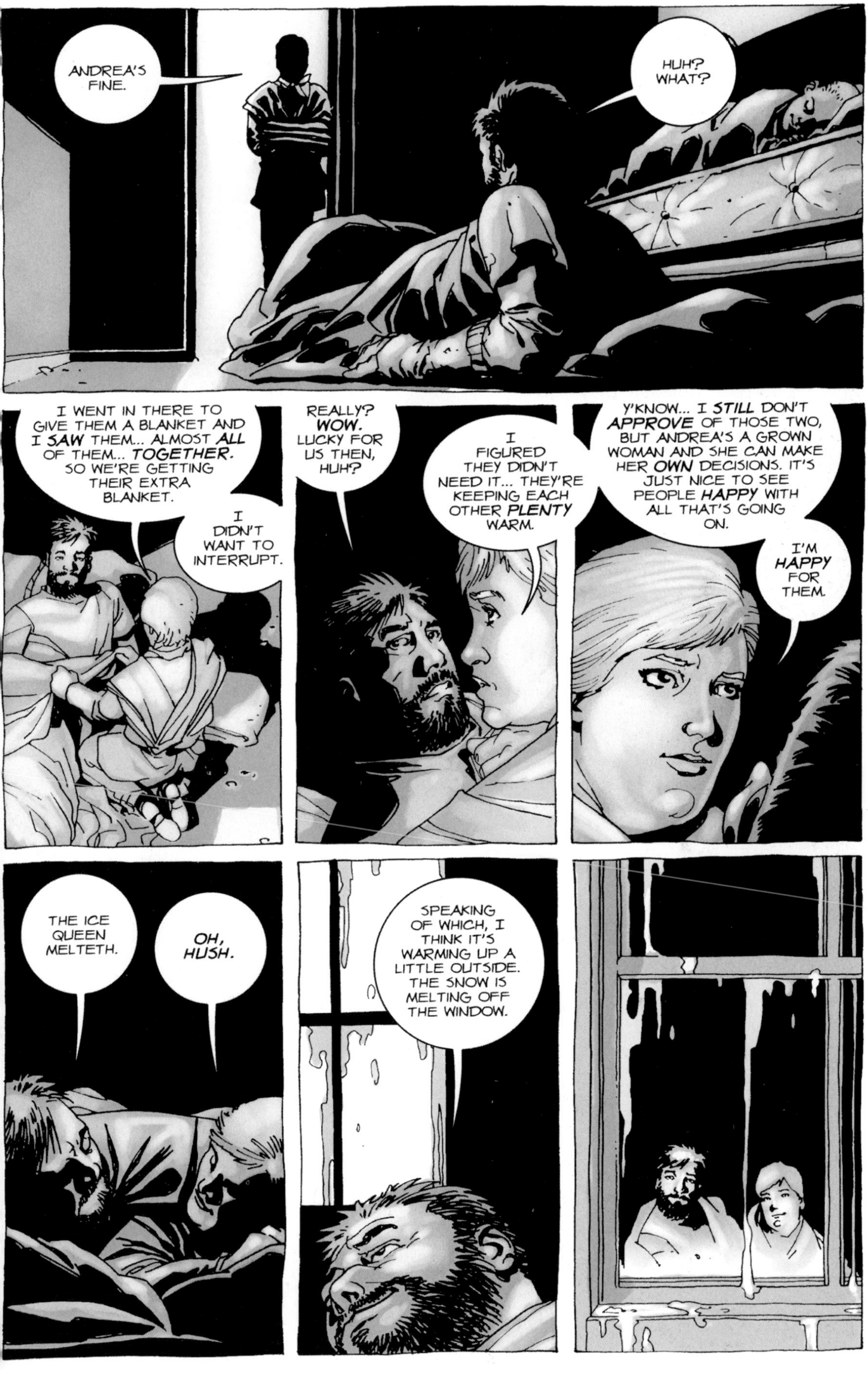
ANDREA'S FINE.
HUH? WHAT?
I WENT IN THERE TO GIVE THEM A BLANKET AND I SAW THEM... ALMOST ALL OF THEM... TOGETHER. SO WE'RE GETTING THEIR EXTRA BLANKET.
I DIDN'T WANT TO INTERRUPT.
REALLY? WOW. LUCKY FOR US THEN, HUH?
I FIGURED THEY DIDN'T NEED IT... THEY'RE KEEPING EACH OTHER PLENTY WARM.
Y'KNOW... I STILL DON'T APPROVE OF THOSE TWO, BUT ANDREA'S A GROWN WOMAN AND SHE CAN MAKE HER OWN DECISIONS. IT'S JUST NICE TO SEE PEOPLE HAPPY WITH ALL THAT'S GOING ON.
I'M HAPPY FOR THEM.
THE ICE QUEEN MELTETH.
OH, HUSH.
SPEAKING OF WHICH, I THINK IT'S WARMING UP A LITTLE OUTSIDE. THE SNOW IS MELTING OFF THE WINDOW.

PLOP

PLOP

PLOP

PLOP

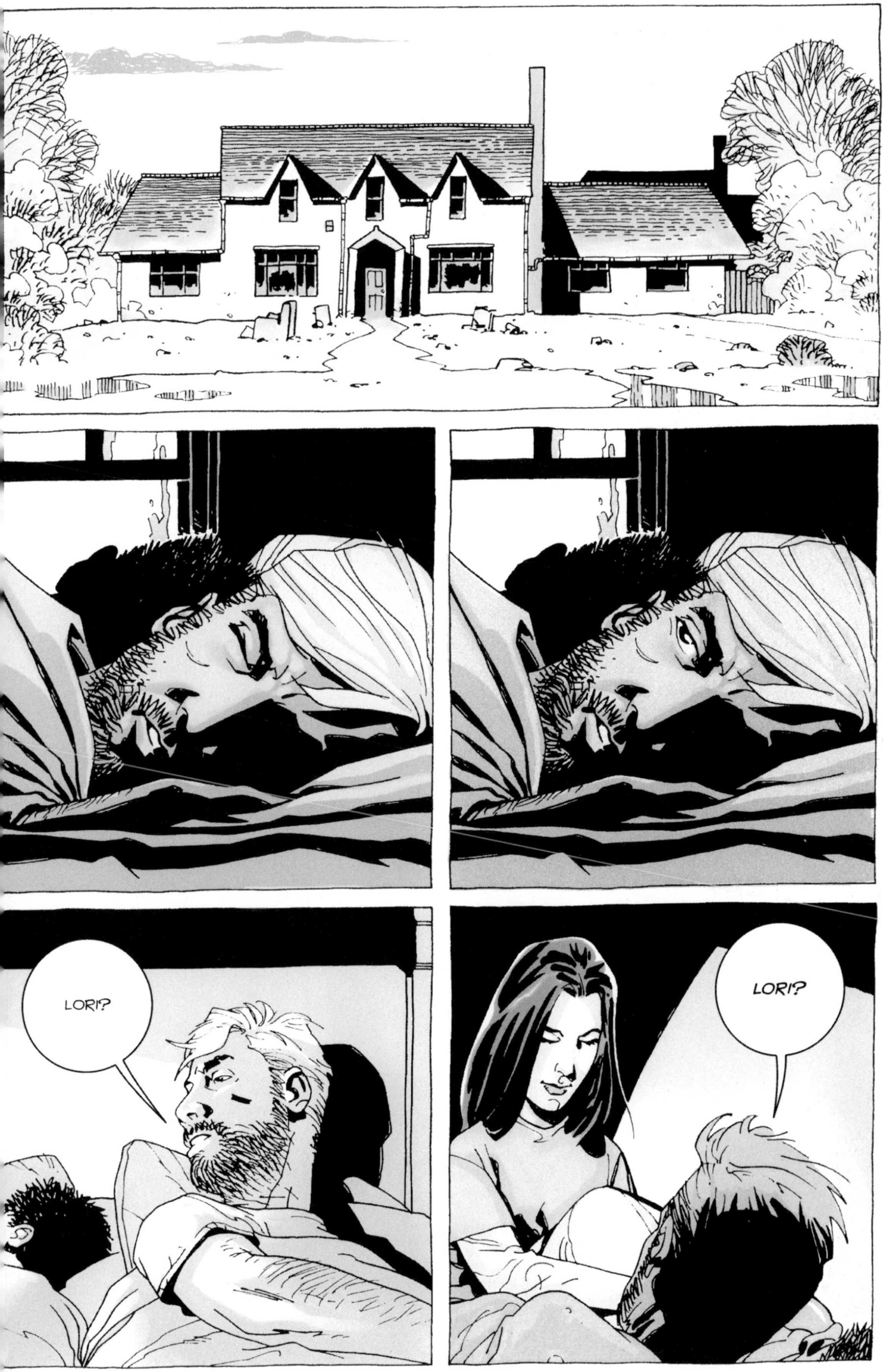
LORI?
LORI?

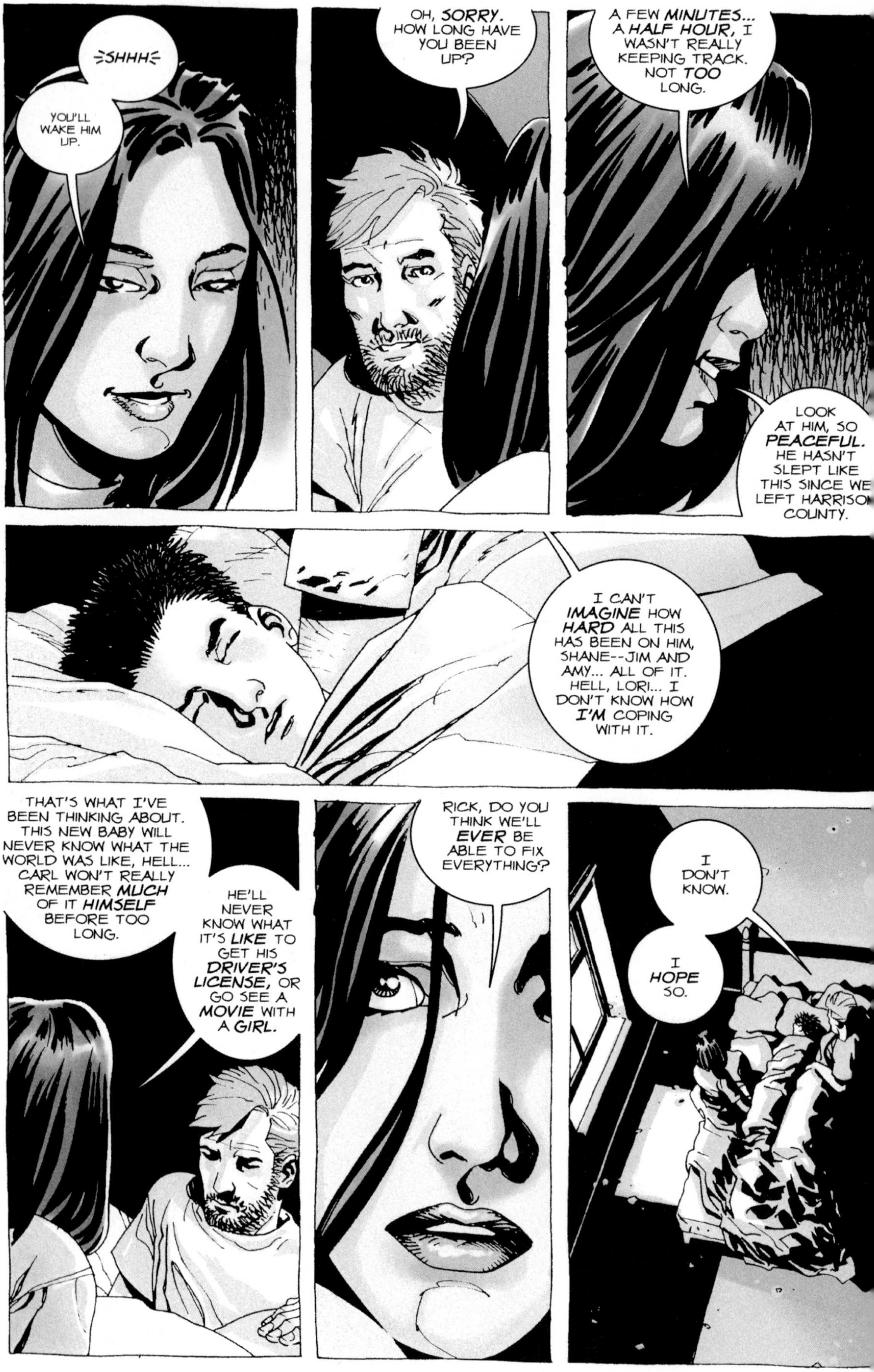

SHHH
YOU'LL WAKE HIM UP.
OH, SORRY. HOW LONG HAVE YOU BEEN UP?
A FEW MINUTES... A HALF HOUR, I WASN'T REALLY KEEPING TRACK. NOT TOO LONG.
LOOK AT HIM, SO PEACEFUL. HE HASN'T SLEPT LIKE THIS SINCE WE LEFT HARRISON COUNTY.
I CAN'T IMAGINE HOW HARD ALL THIS HAS BEEN ON HIM, SHANE--JIM AND AMY... ALL OF IT. HELL, LORI... I DON'T KNOW HOW I'M COPING WITH IT.
THAT'S WHAT I'VE BEEN THINKING ABOUT. THIS NEW BABY WILL NEVER KNOW WHAT THE WORLD WAS LIKE, HELL... CARL WON'T REALLY REMEMBER MUCH OF IT HIMSELF BEFORE TOO LONG.
HE'LL NEVER KNOW WHAT IT'S LIKE TO GET HIS DRIVER'S LICENSE, OR GO SEE A MOVIE WITH A GIRL.
RICK, DO YOU THINK WE'LL EVER BE ABLE TO FIX EVERYTHING?
I DON'T KNOW.
I HOPE SO.

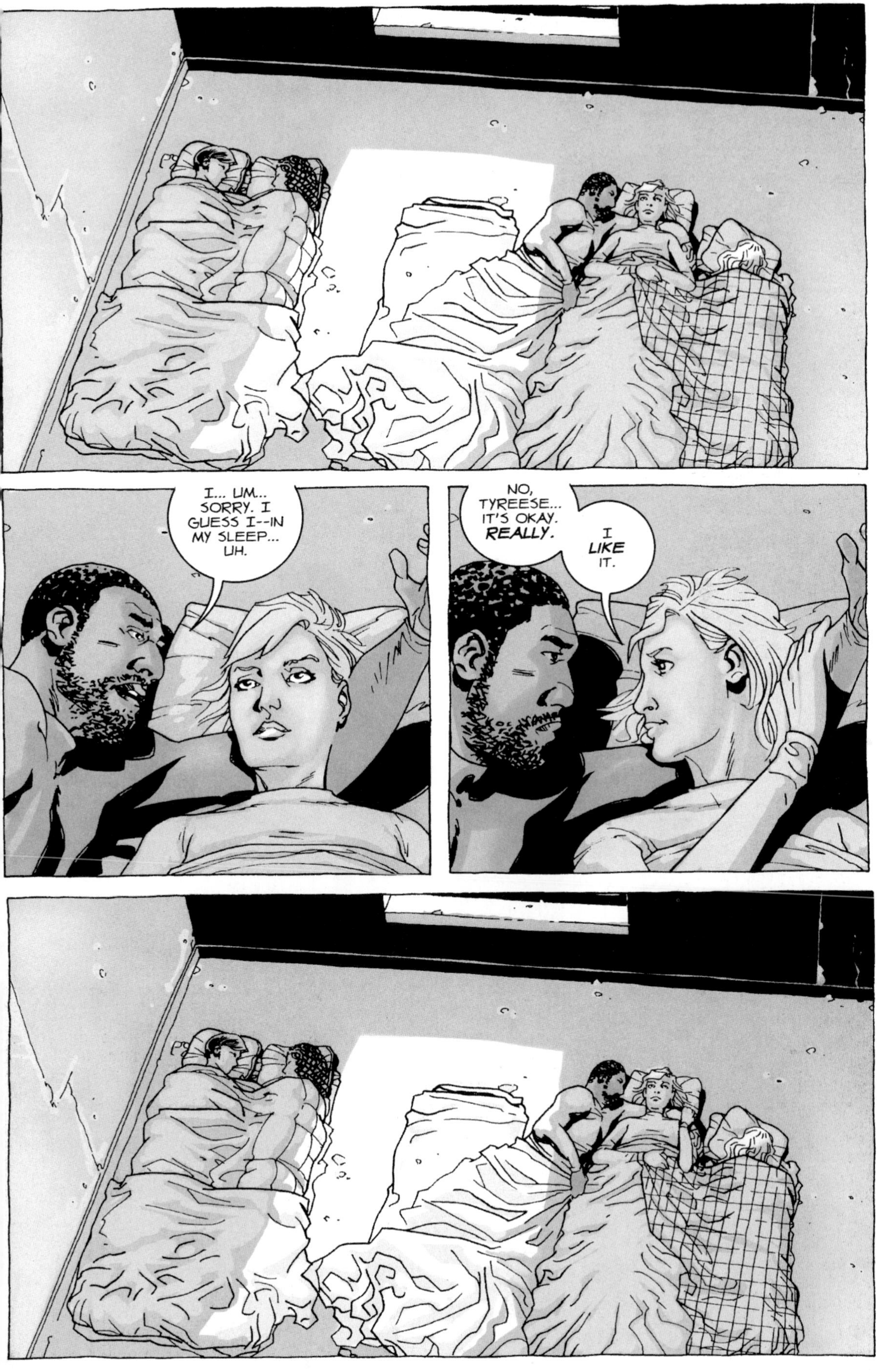
I... UM... SORRY. I GUESS I--IN MY SLEEP... UH.
NO, TYREESE... IT'S OKAY. REALLY.
I LIKE IT.

WHAT ARE YOU *THINKING?*

I DIDN'T KNOW YOU WERE AWAKE.

SURPRISE.

I WAS JUST THINKING ABOUT ANDREA AND DALE... THEY BOTH LOST SOMEONE THEY *LOVED...* SOMEONE VERY *CLOSE* TO THEM. IT HIT THEM HARD, WE SAW THAT... BUT THEY EVENTUALLY PULLED OUT OF IT. SEEING THEM *TOGETHER* LAST NIGHT-- THEY'RE *HAPPY.*

SEEING THEM--KNOWING THAT THEY CAN PUT THEIR LIVES BACK TOGETHER... IT GIVES ME *HOPE.*

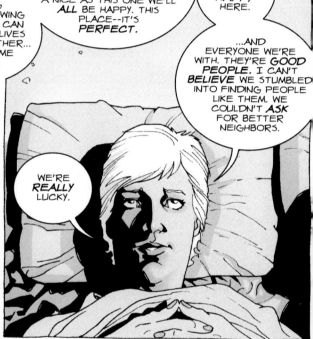

AND THEN THERE'S *THIS* PLACE... A CHANCE TO *START OVER.* A NEW PLACE... ALL TO OURSELVES, AND IF *HALF* OF THE HOUSES IN THIS NEIGHBORHOOD ARE AS NICE AS THIS ONE WE'LL *ALL* BE HAPPY. THIS PLACE--IT'S *PERFECT.*

I THINK WE CAN BE *HAPPY* HERE.

...AND EVERYONE WE'RE WITH. THEY'RE *GOOD PEOPLE.* I CAN'T *BELIEVE* WE STUMBLED INTO FINDING PEOPLE LIKE THEM. WE COULDN'T *ASK* FOR BETTER NEIGHBORS.

WE'RE *REALLY* LUCKY.

YOU'RE *RIGHT.* IF THIS WORKS OUT WE'VE GOT IT *MADE.* IT'S BEEN A WHILE SINCE I'VE SEEN YOU THIS HAPPY, *DONNA.*

YOU WANT TO HAVE *SEX?*

WHAT'S A *SEGS?*

THAT ANSWER YOUR QUESTION?

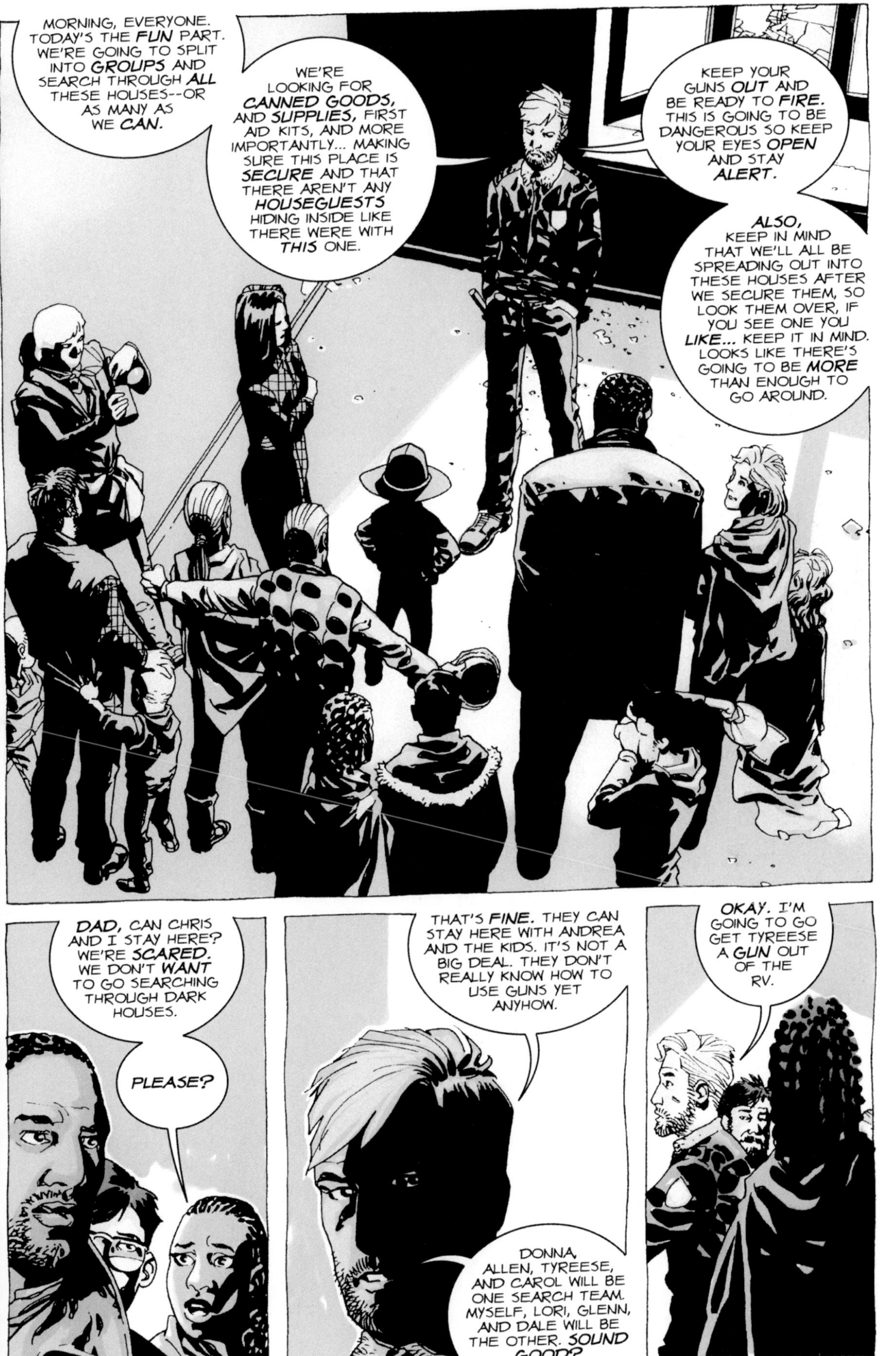
MORNING, EVERYONE. TODAY'S THE FUN PART. WE'RE GOING TO SPLIT INTO GROUPS AND SEARCH THROUGH ALL THESE HOUSES--OR AS MANY AS WE CAN.
WE'RE LOOKING FOR CANNED GOODS, AND SUPPLIES, FIRST AID KITS, AND MORE IMPORTANTLY... MAKING SURE THIS PLACE IS SECURE AND THAT THERE AREN'T ANY HOUSEGUESTS HIDING INSIDE LIKE THERE WERE WITH THIS ONE.
KEEP YOUR GUNS OUT AND BE READY TO FIRE. THIS IS GOING TO BE DANGEROUS SO KEEP YOUR EYES OPEN AND STAY ALERT.
ALSO, KEEP IN MIND THAT WE'LL ALL BE SPREADING OUT INTO THESE HOUSES AFTER WE SECURE THEM, SO LOOK THEM OVER, IF YOU SEE ONE YOU LIKE... KEEP IT IN MIND. LOOKS LIKE THERE'S GOING TO BE MORE THAN ENOUGH TO GO AROUND.
DAD, CAN CHRIS AND I STAY HERE? WE'RE SCARED. WE DON'T WANT TO GO SEARCHING THROUGH DARK HOUSES.
PLEASE?
THAT'S FINE. THEY CAN STAY HERE WITH ANDREA AND THE KIDS. IT'S NOT A BIG DEAL. THEY DON'T REALLY KNOW HOW TO USE GUNS YET ANYHOW.
DONNA, ALLEN, TYREESE, AND CAROL WILL BE ONE SEARCH TEAM. MYSELF, LORI, GLENN, AND DALE WILL BE THE OTHER. SOUND GOOD?
OKAY. I'M GOING TO GO GET TYREESE A GUN OUT OF THE RV.

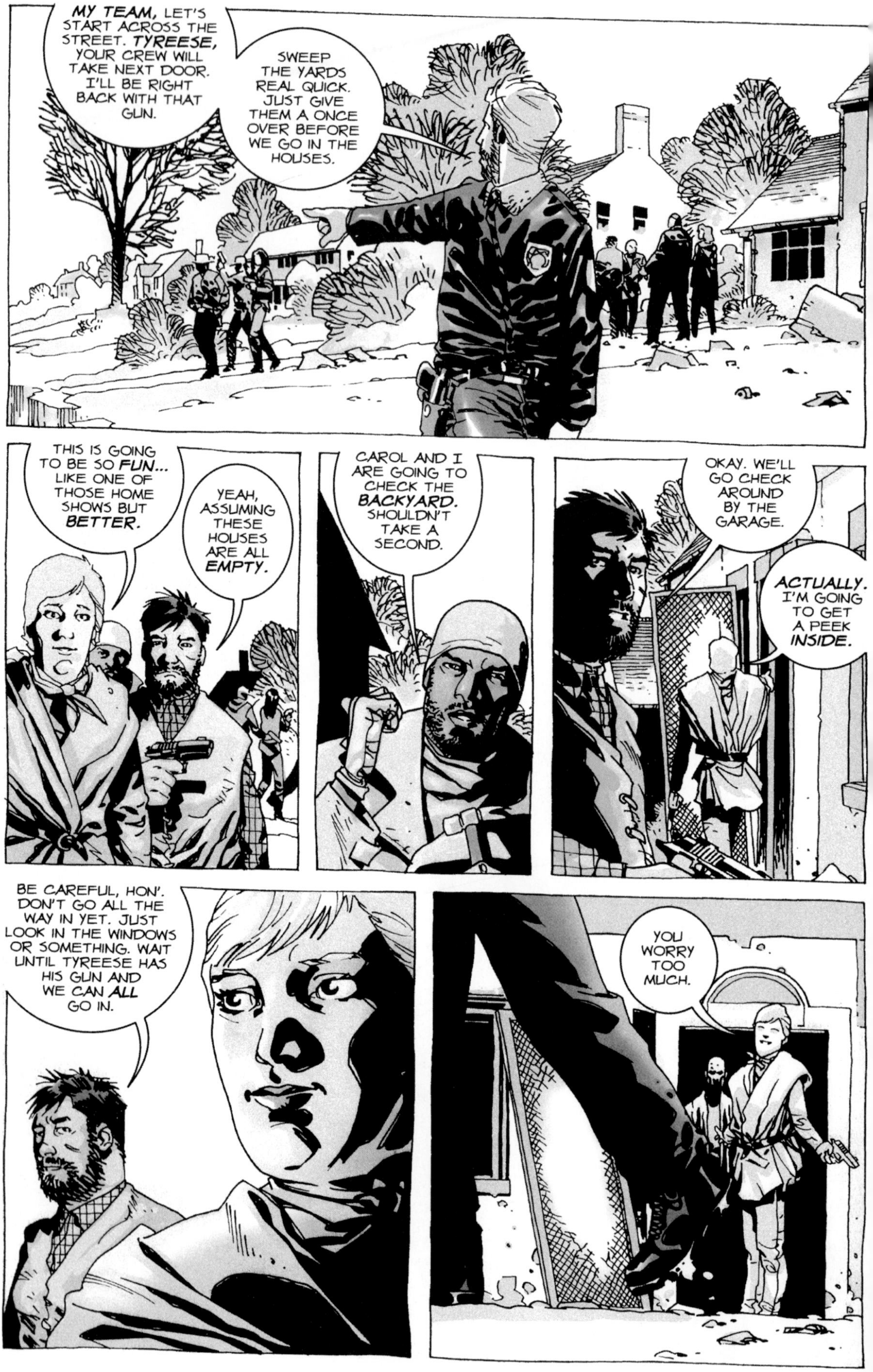
MY TEAM, LET'S START ACROSS THE STREET. TYREESE, YOUR CREW WILL TAKE NEXT DOOR. I'LL BE RIGHT BACK WITH THAT GUN.
SWEEP THE YARDS REAL QUICK. JUST GIVE THEM A ONCE OVER BEFORE WE GO IN THE HOUSES.
THIS IS GOING TO BE SO FUN... LIKE ONE OF THOSE HOME SHOWS BUT BETTER.
YEAH, ASSUMING THESE HOUSES ARE ALL EMPTY.
CAROL AND I ARE GOING TO CHECK THE BACKYARD. SHOULDN'T TAKE A SECOND.
OKAY. WE'LL GO CHECK AROUND BY THE GARAGE.
ACTUALLY. I'M GOING TO GET A PEEK INSIDE.
BE CAREFUL, HON'. DON'T GO ALL THE WAY IN YET. JUST LOOK IN THE WINDOWS OR SOMETHING. WAIT UNTIL TYREESE HAS HIS GUN AND WE CAN ALL GO IN.
YOU WORRY TOO MUCH.

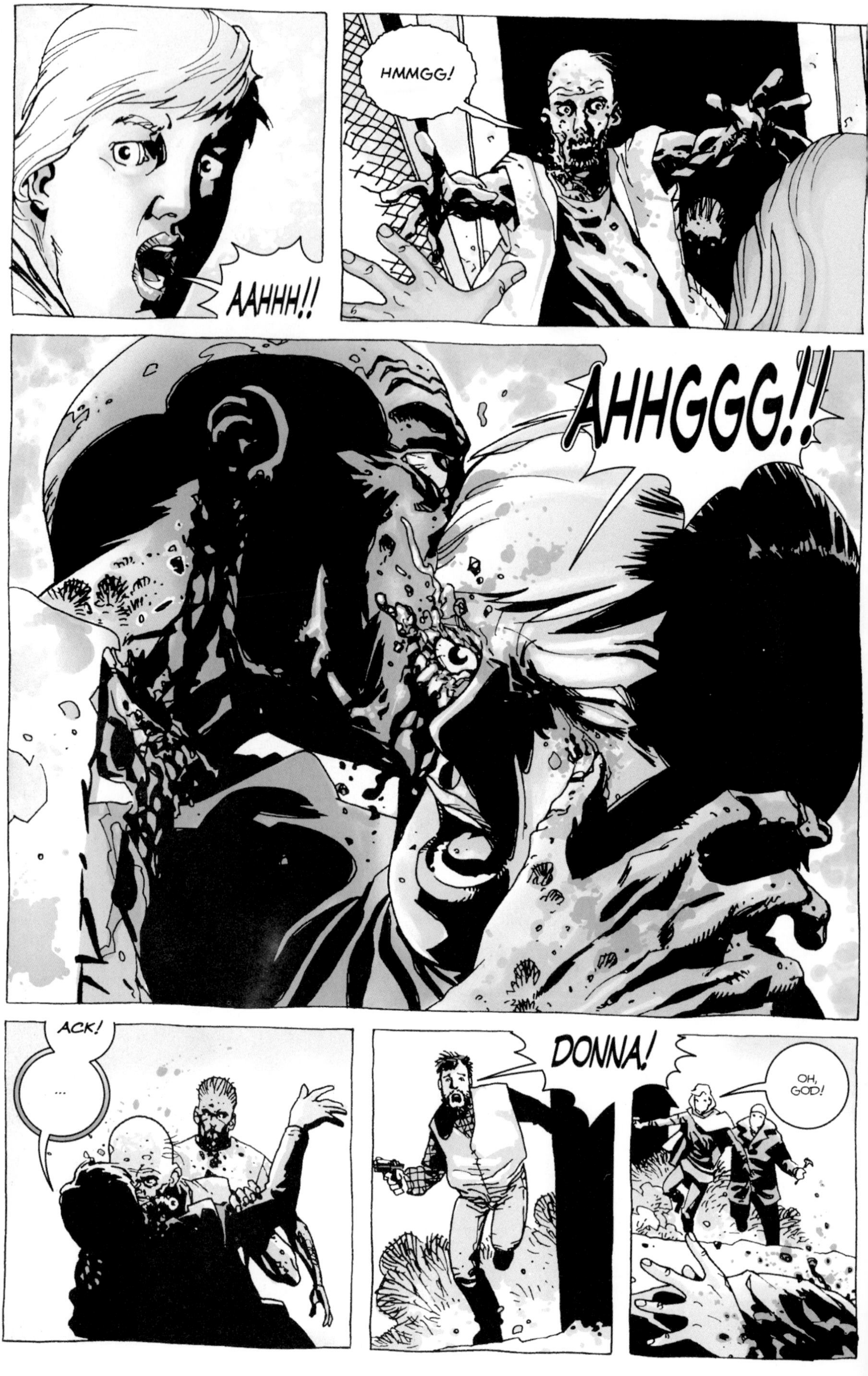
AAHHH!!
HMMGG!
AHHGGG!!
ACK!
...
DONNA!
OH, GOD!

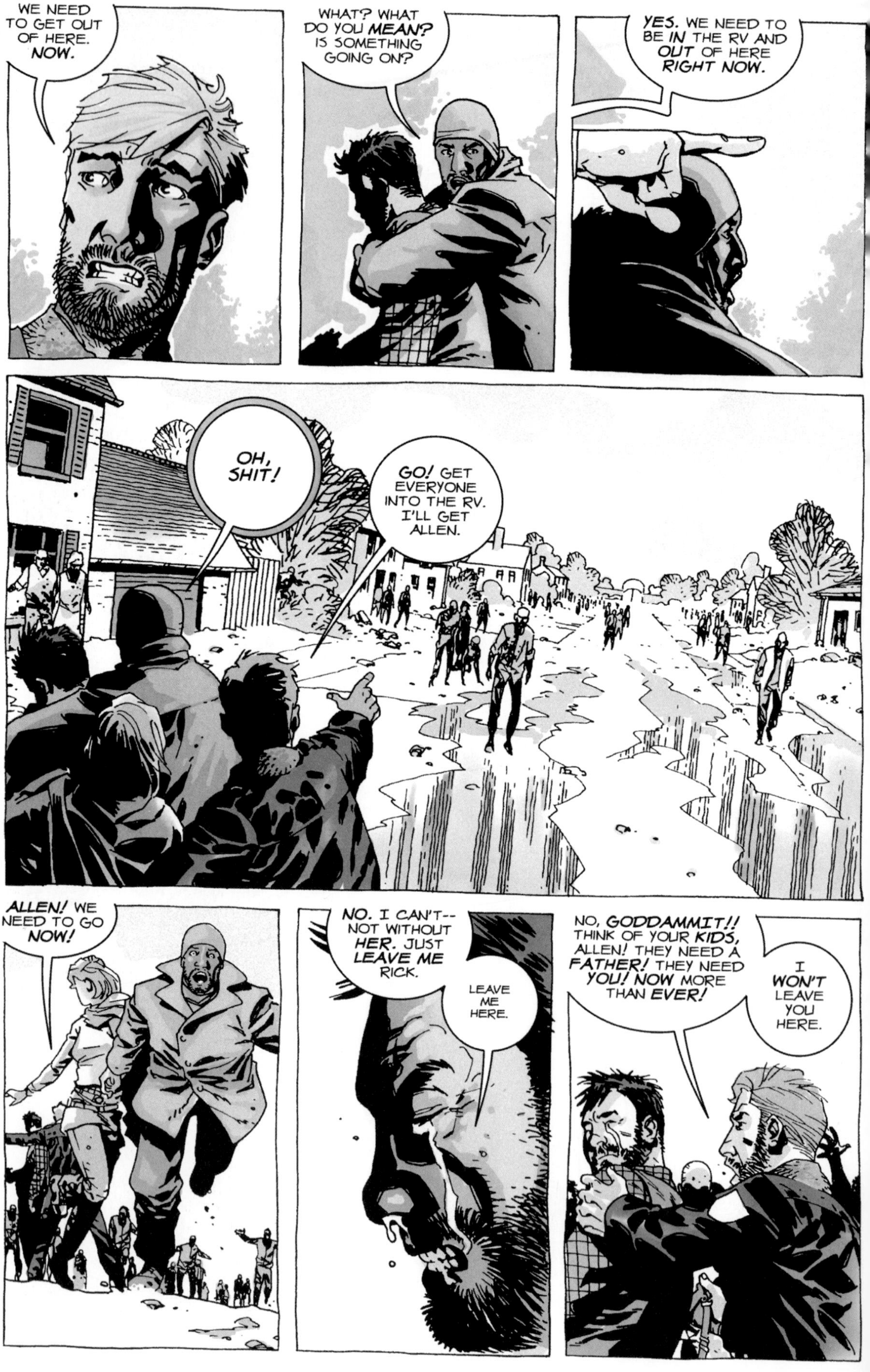

WE NEED TO GET OUT OF HERE. NOW.
WHAT? WHAT DO YOU MEAN? IS SOMETHING GOING ON?
YES. WE NEED TO BE IN THE RV AND OUT OF HERE RIGHT NOW.
OH, SHIT!
GO! GET EVERYONE INTO THE RV. I'LL GET ALLEN.
ALLEN! WE NEED TO GO NOW!
NO. I CAN'T-- NOT WITHOUT HER. JUST LEAVE ME RICK.
LEAVE ME HERE.
NO, GODDAMMIT!! THINK OF YOUR KIDS, ALLEN! THEY NEED A FATHER! THEY NEED YOU! NOW MORE THAN EVER!
I WON'T LEAVE YOU HERE.

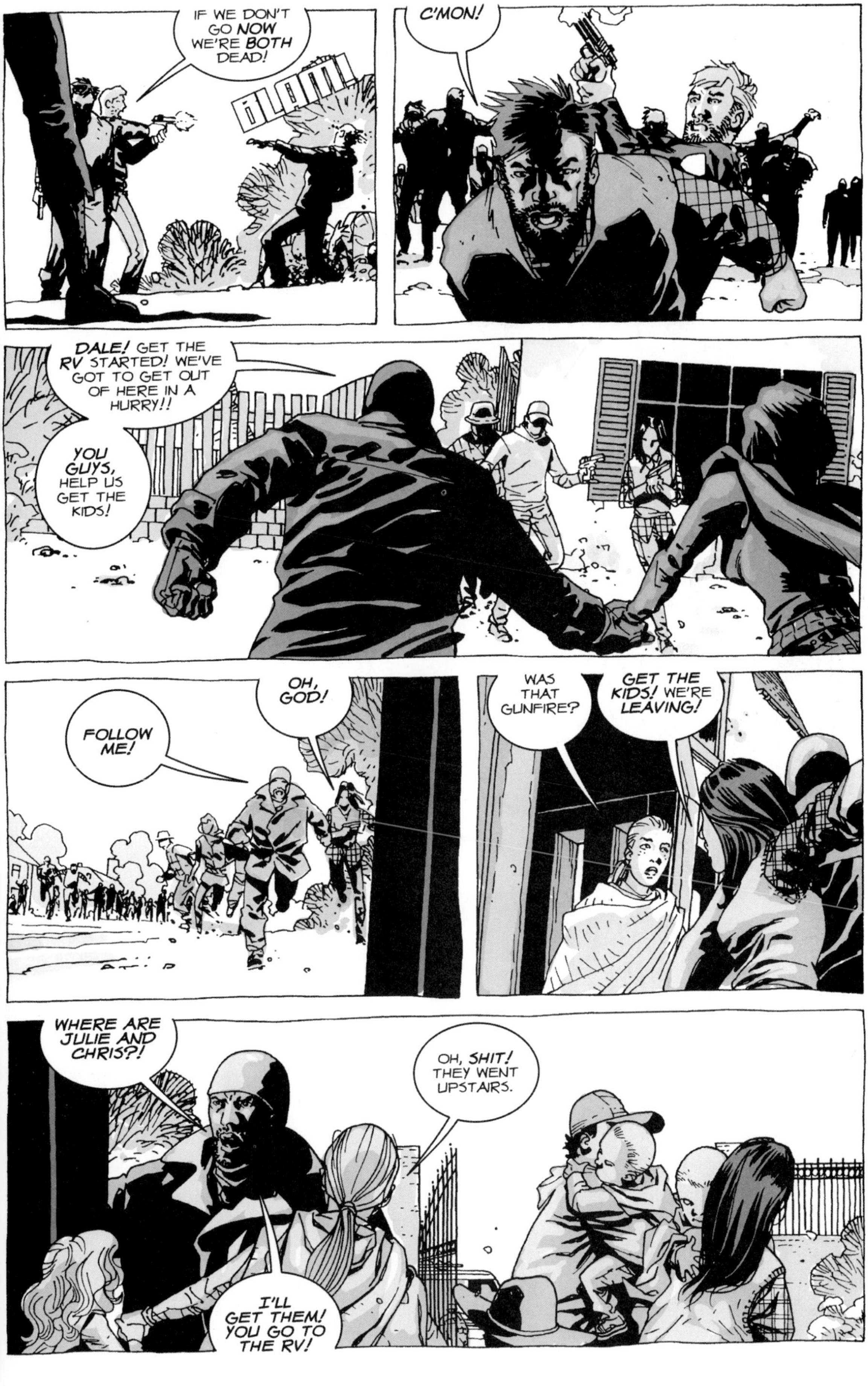
IF WE DON'T GO NOW WE'RE BOTH DEAD!
BLAM
C'MON!
DALE! GET THE RV STARTED! WE'VE GOT TO GET OUT OF HERE IN A HURRY!!
YOU GUYS, HELP US GET THE KIDS!
FOLLOW ME!
OH, GOD!
WAS THAT GUNFIRE?
GET THE KIDS! WE'RE LEAVING!
WHERE ARE JULIE AND CHRIS?!
OH, SHIT! THEY WENT UPSTAIRS.
I'LL GET THEM! YOU GO TO THE RV!

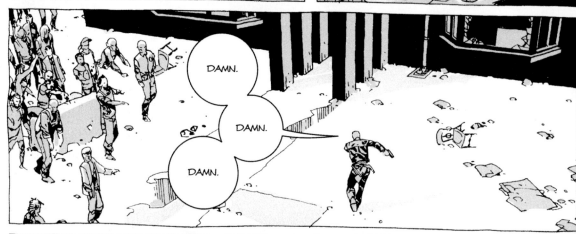

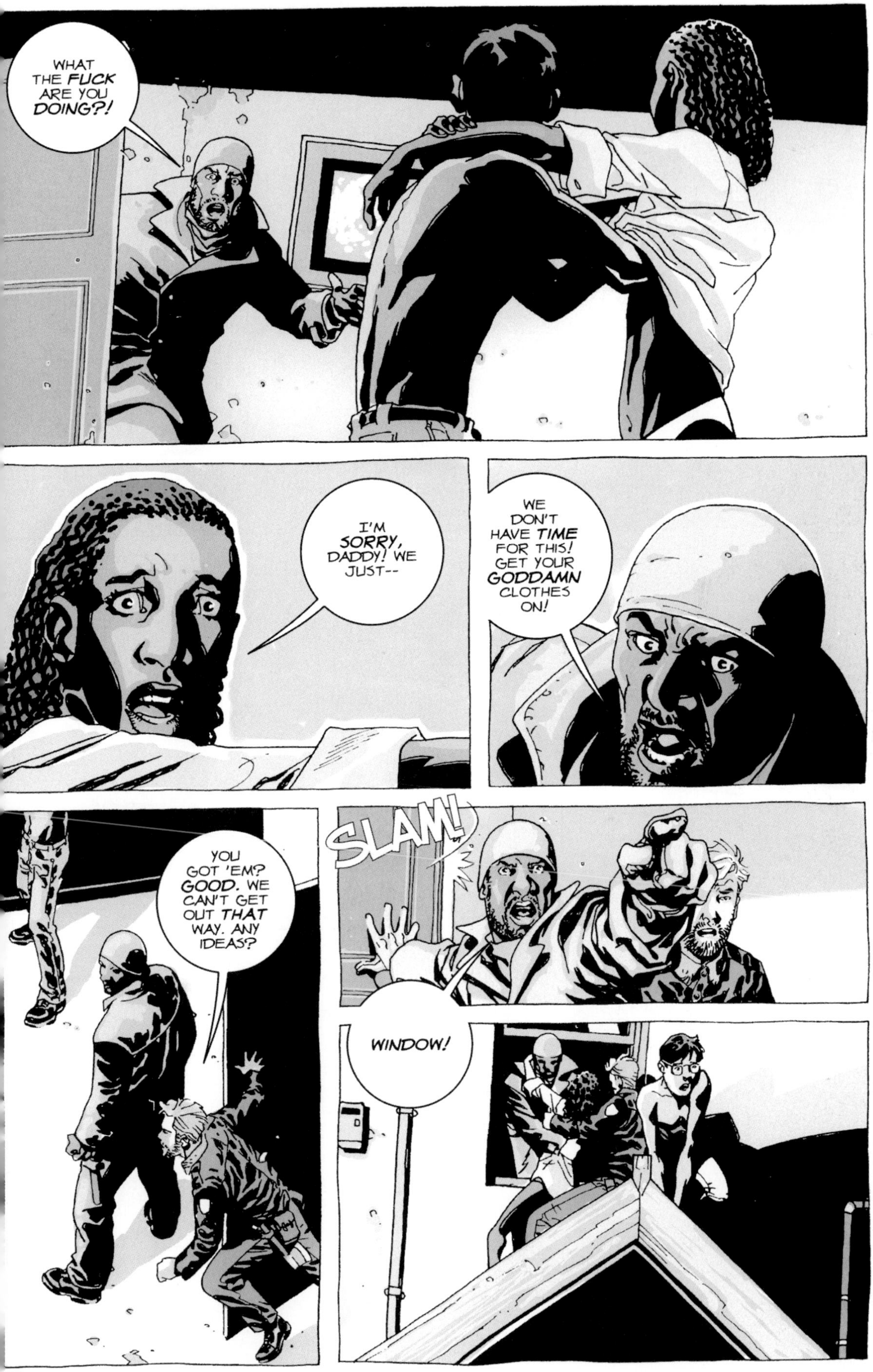
WHAT THE FUCK ARE YOU DOING?!
I'M SORRY, DADDY! WE JUST--
WE DON'T HAVE TIME FOR THIS! GET YOUR GODDAMN CLOTHES ON!
YOU GOT 'EM? GOOD. WE CAN'T GET OUT THAT WAY. ANY IDEAS?
SLAM!
WINDOW!

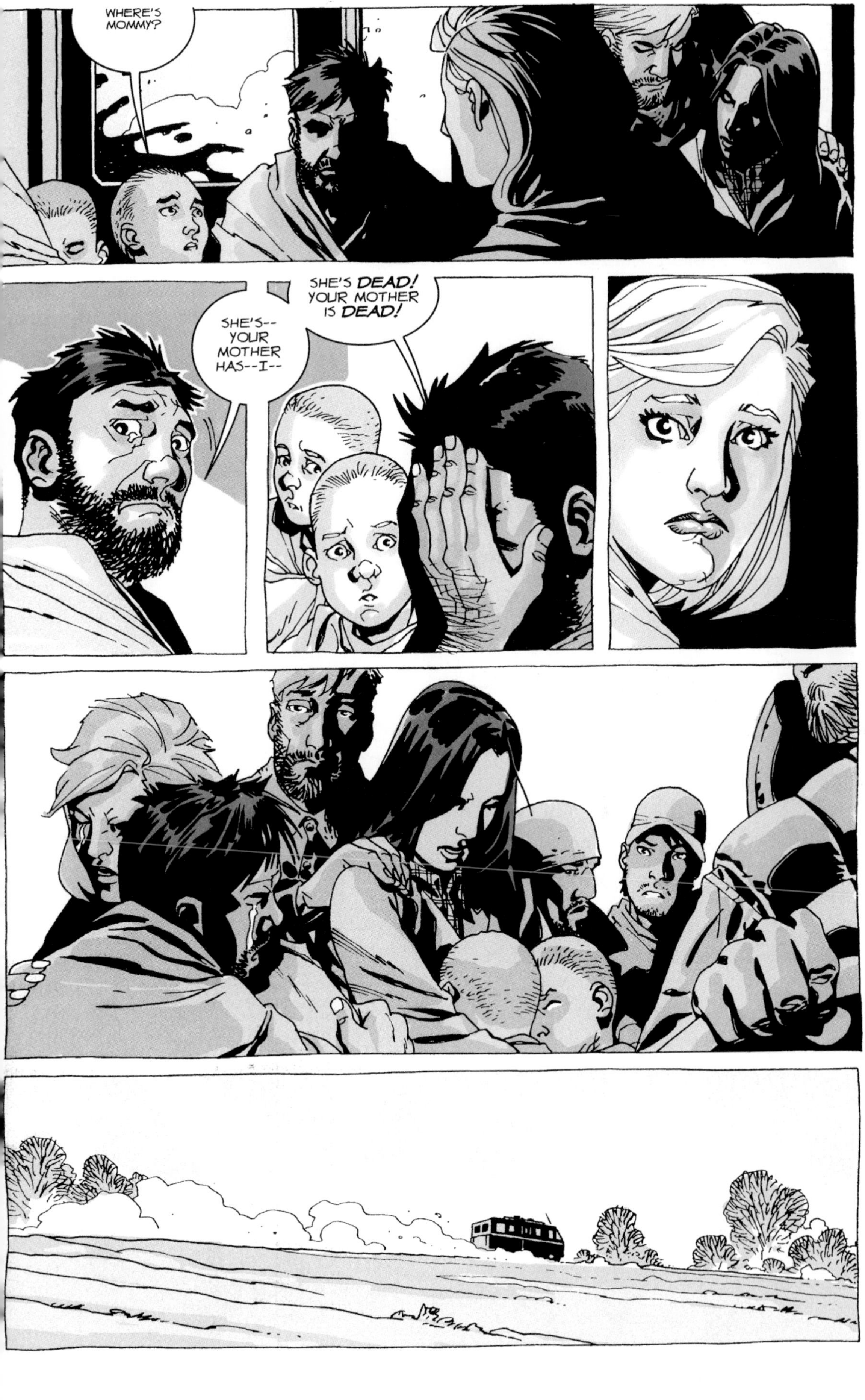
WHERE'S MOMMY?
SHE'S-- YOUR MOTHER HAS--I--
SHE'S DEAD! YOUR MOTHER IS DEAD!

BE CAREFUL GUYS... BE READY FOR *ANYTHING.*

DAMN.

ANYTHING THAT WASN'T TAKEN WAS *DESTROYED.* WHY THE *HELL* WOULD ANYONE *DO* THIS?

WHO KNOWS... *SHIT.* THIS IS NOT *GOOD.*

HOW THE *HELL* ARE WE GOING TO MAKE IT WITHOUT ANY *FOOD?*

I SEE LOTS OF *HUNTING* IN OUR FUTURE.

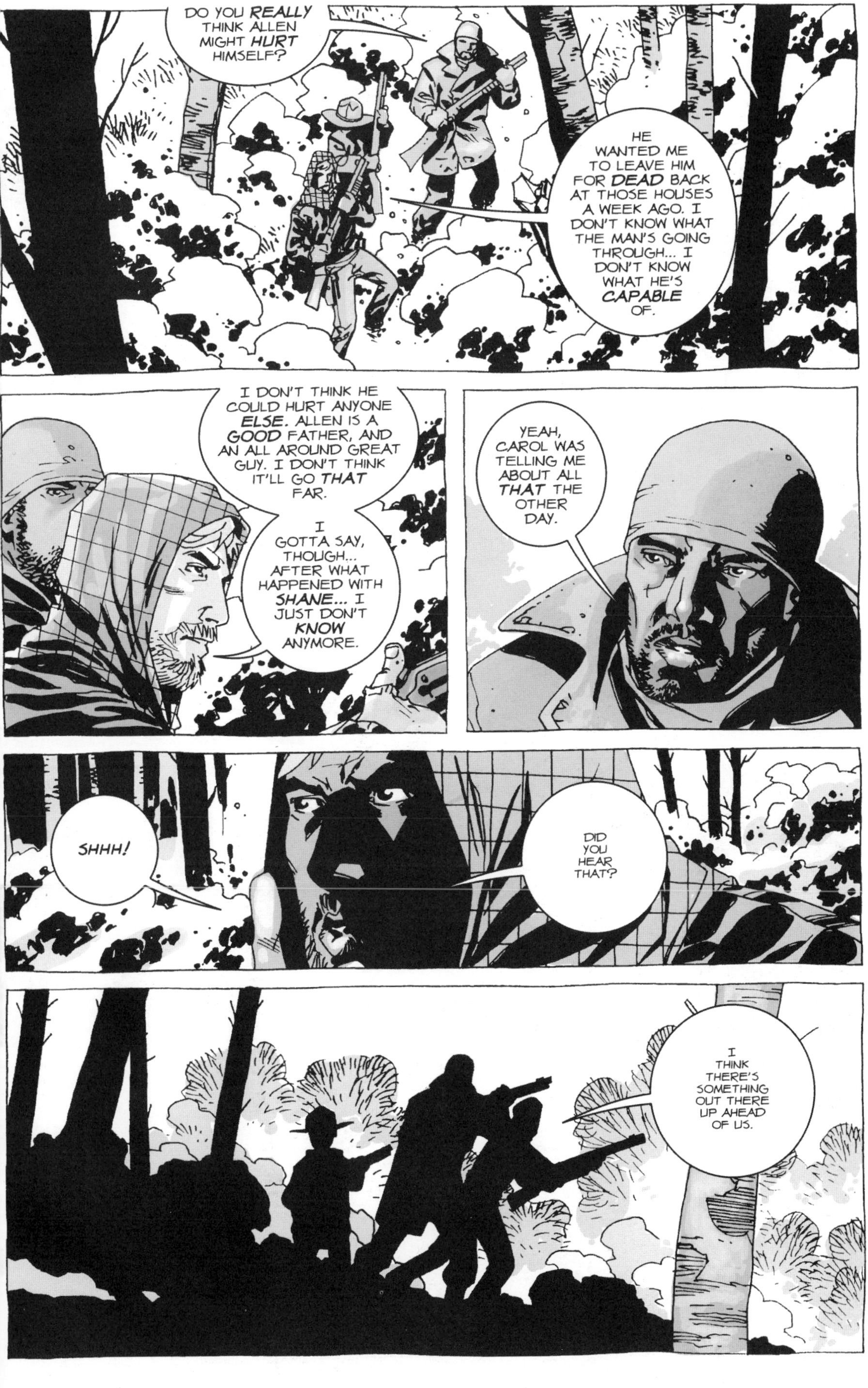
DO YOU REALLY THINK ALLEN MIGHT HURT HIMSELF?
HE WANTED ME TO LEAVE HIM FOR DEAD BACK AT THOSE HOUSES A WEEK AGO. I DON'T KNOW WHAT THE MAN'S GOING THROUGH... I DON'T KNOW WHAT HE'S CAPABLE OF.
I DON'T THINK HE COULD HURT ANYONE ELSE. ALLEN IS A GOOD FATHER, AND AN ALL AROUND GREAT GUY. I DON'T THINK IT'LL GO THAT FAR.
I GOTTA SAY, THOUGH... AFTER WHAT HAPPENED WITH SHANE... I JUST DON'T KNOW ANYMORE.
YEAH, CAROL WAS TELLING ME ABOUT ALL THAT THE OTHER DAY.
SHHH!
DID YOU HEAR THAT?
I THINK THERE'S SOMETHING OUT THERE UP AHEAD OF US.

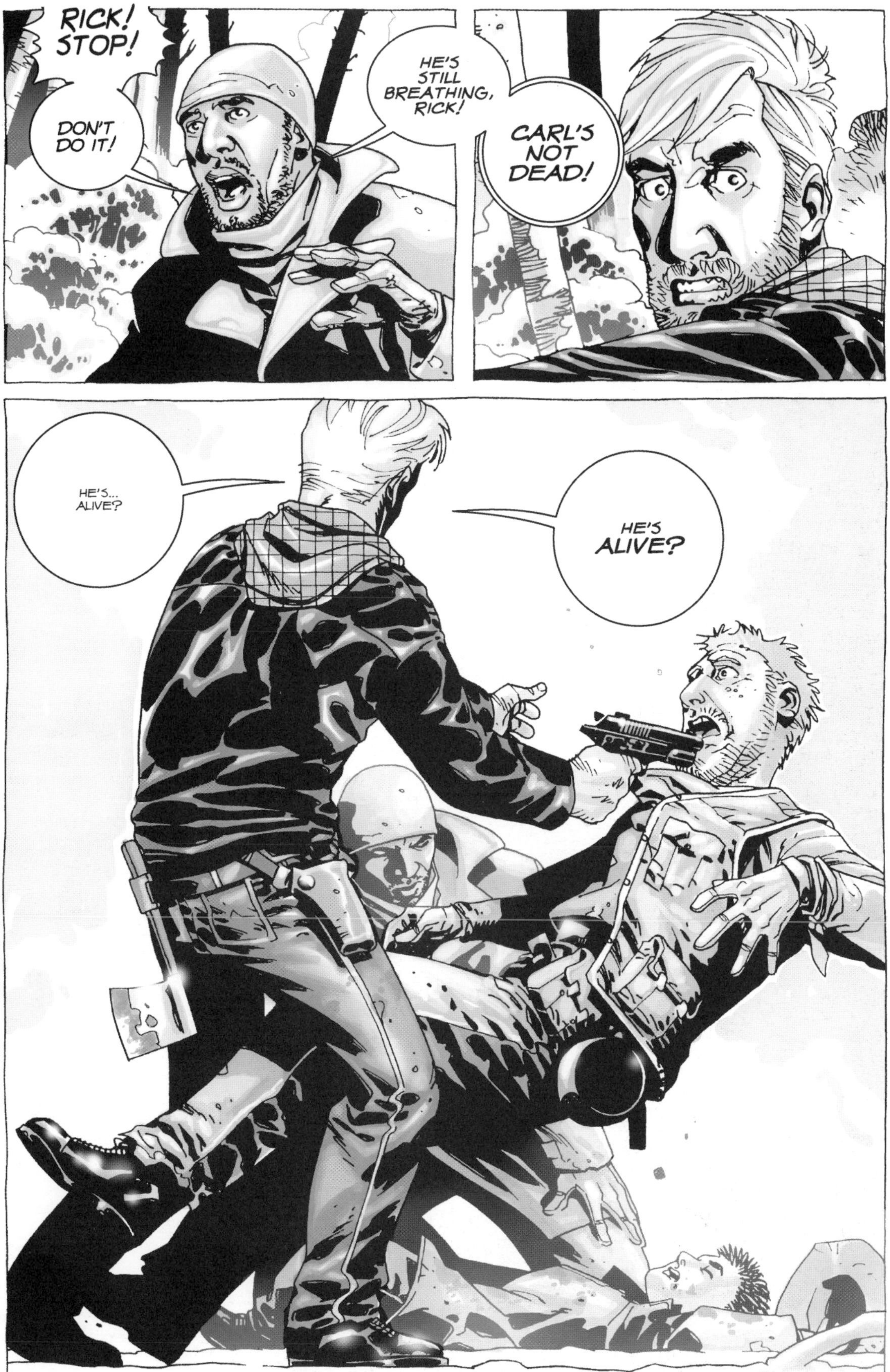
RICK! STOP!
DON'T DO IT!
HE'S STILL BREATHING, RICK!
CARL'S NOT DEAD!
HE'S... ALIVE?
HE'S ALIVE?

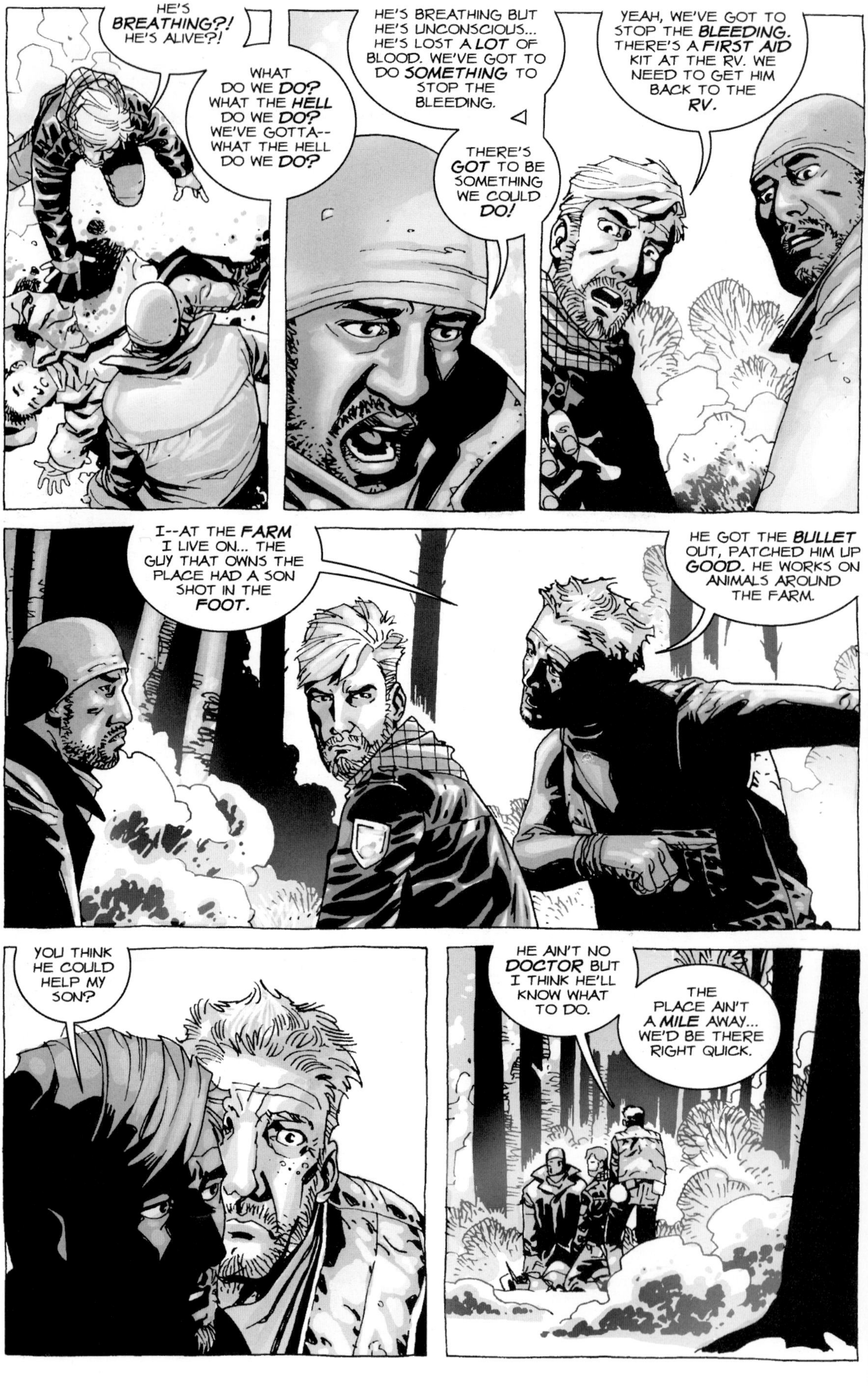

HE'S BREATHING?! HE'S ALIVE?!
WHAT DO WE DO? WHAT THE HELL DO WE DO? WE'VE GOTTA-- WHAT THE HELL DO WE DO?
HE'S BREATHING BUT HE'S UNCONSCIOUS... HE'S LOST A LOT OF BLOOD. WE'VE GOT TO DO SOMETHING TO STOP THE BLEEDING.
THERE'S GOT TO BE SOMETHING WE COULD DO!
YEAH, WE'VE GOT TO STOP THE BLEEDING. THERE'S A FIRST AID KIT AT THE RV. WE NEED TO GET HIM BACK TO THE RV.
I--AT THE FARM I LIVE ON... THE GUY THAT OWNS THE PLACE HAD A SON SHOT IN THE FOOT.
HE GOT THE BULLET OUT, PATCHED HIM UP GOOD. HE WORKS ON ANIMALS AROUND THE FARM.
YOU THINK HE COULD HELP MY SON?
HE AIN'T NO DOCTOR BUT I THINK HE'LL KNOW WHAT TO DO.
THE PLACE AIN'T A MILE AWAY... WE'D BE THERE RIGHT QUICK.

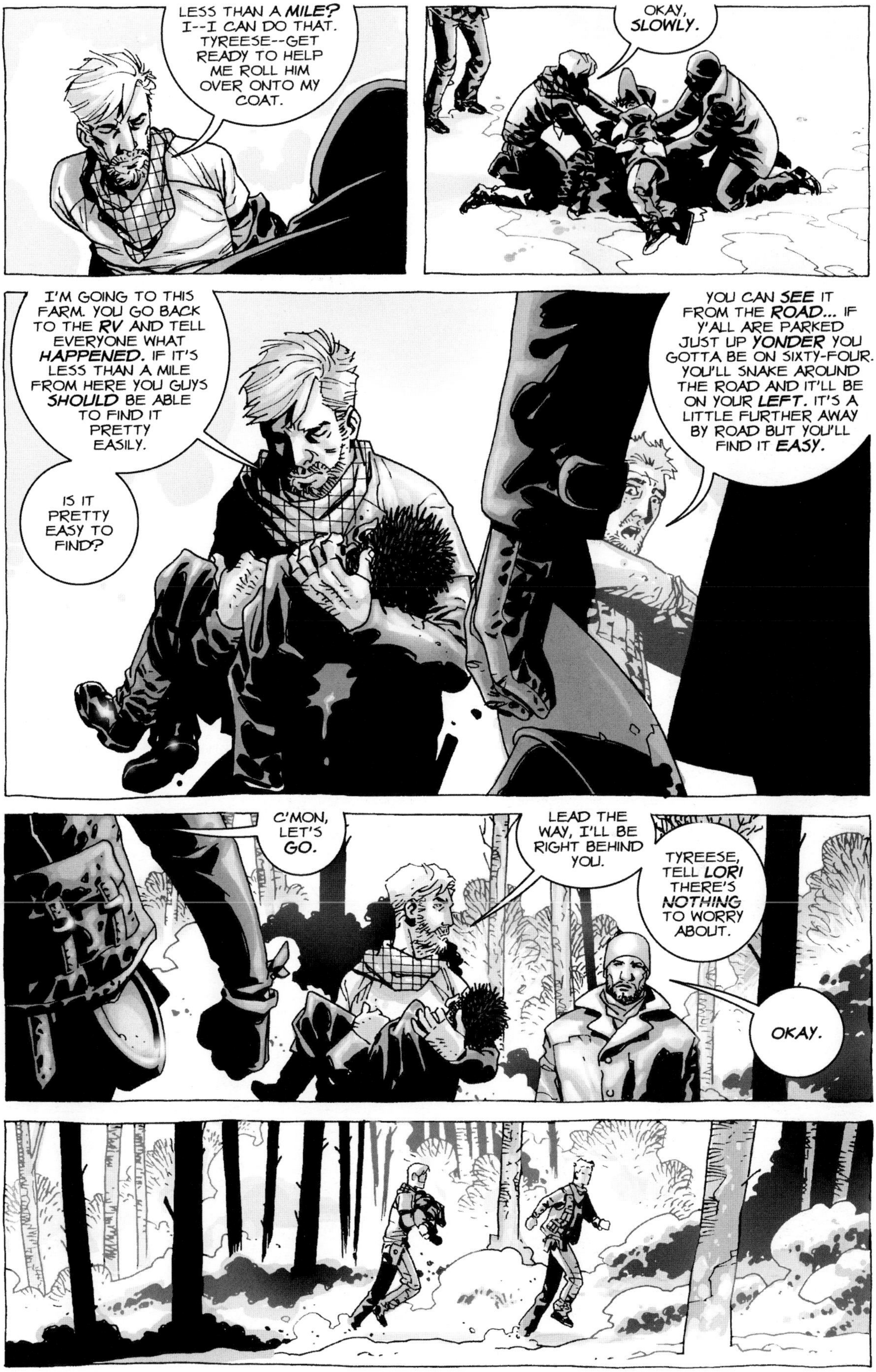
LESS THAN A MILE? I--I CAN DO THAT. TYREESE--GET READY TO HELP ME ROLL HIM OVER ONTO MY COAT.
OKAY, SLOWLY.
I'M GOING TO THIS FARM. YOU GO BACK TO THE RV AND TELL EVERYONE WHAT HAPPENED. IF IT'S LESS THAN A MILE FROM HERE YOU GUYS SHOULD BE ABLE TO FIND IT PRETTY EASILY.
IS IT PRETTY EASY TO FIND?
YOU CAN SEE IT FROM THE ROAD... IF Y'ALL ARE PARKED JUST UP YONDER YOU GOTTA BE ON SIXTY-FOUR. YOU'LL SNAKE AROUND THE ROAD AND IT'LL BE ON YOUR LEFT. IT'S A LITTLE FURTHER AWAY BY ROAD BUT YOU'LL FIND IT EASY.
C'MON, LET'S GO.
LEAD THE WAY, I'LL BE RIGHT BEHIND YOU.
TYREESE, TELL LORI THERE'S NOTHING TO WORRY ABOUT.
OKAY.

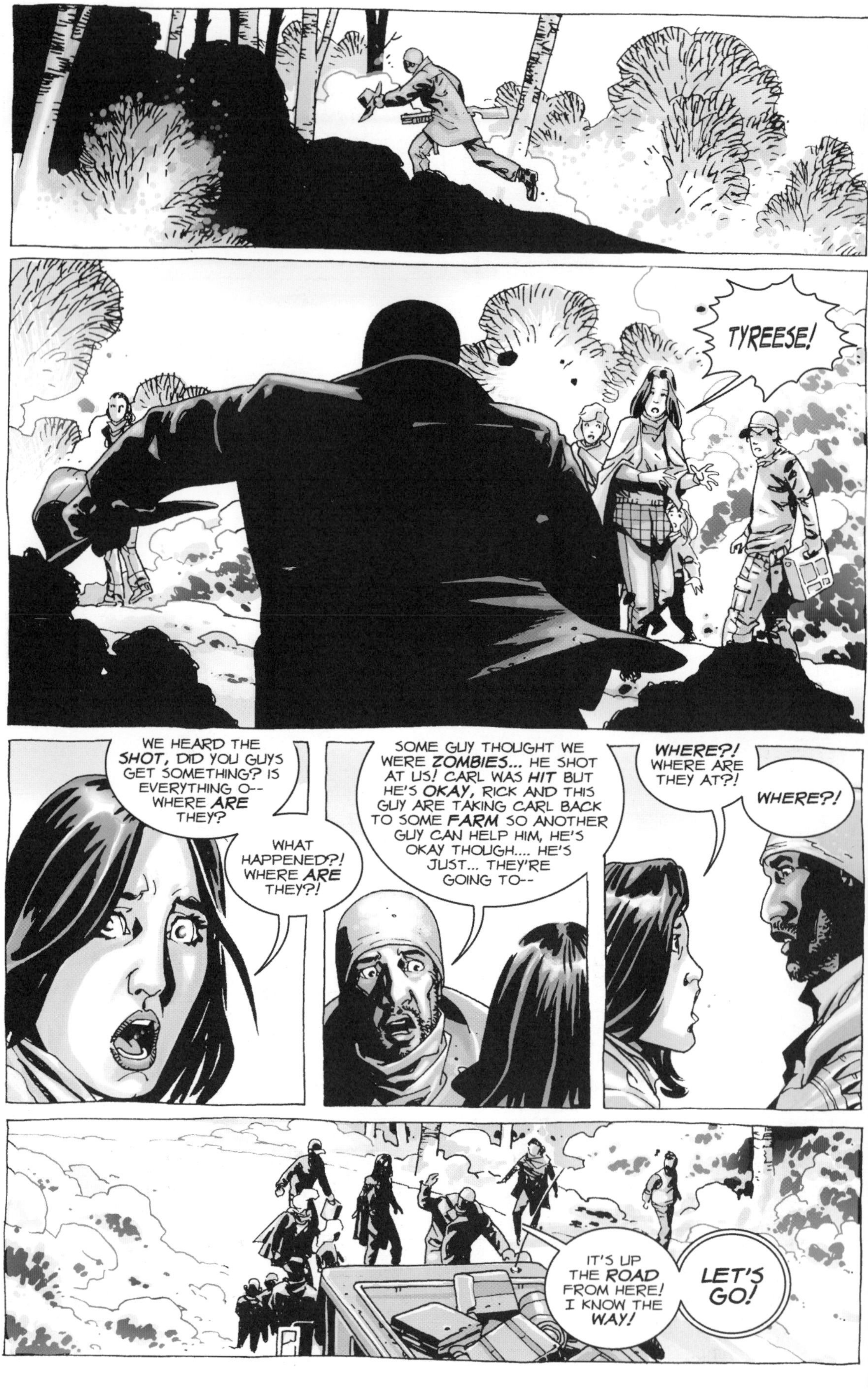
TYREESE!
WE HEARD THE SHOT, DID YOU GUYS GET SOMETHING? IS EVERYTHING O-- WHERE ARE THEY?
WHAT HAPPENED?! WHERE ARE THEY?!
SOME GUY THOUGHT WE WERE ZOMBIES... HE SHOT AT US! CARL WAS HIT BUT HE'S OKAY, RICK AND THIS GUY ARE TAKING CARL BACK TO SOME FARM SO ANOTHER GUY CAN HELP HIM, HE'S OKAY THOUGH.... HE'S JUST... THEY'RE GOING TO--
WHERE?! WHERE ARE THEY AT?!
WHERE?!
IT'S UP THE ROAD FROM HERE! I KNOW THE WAY!
LET'S GO!

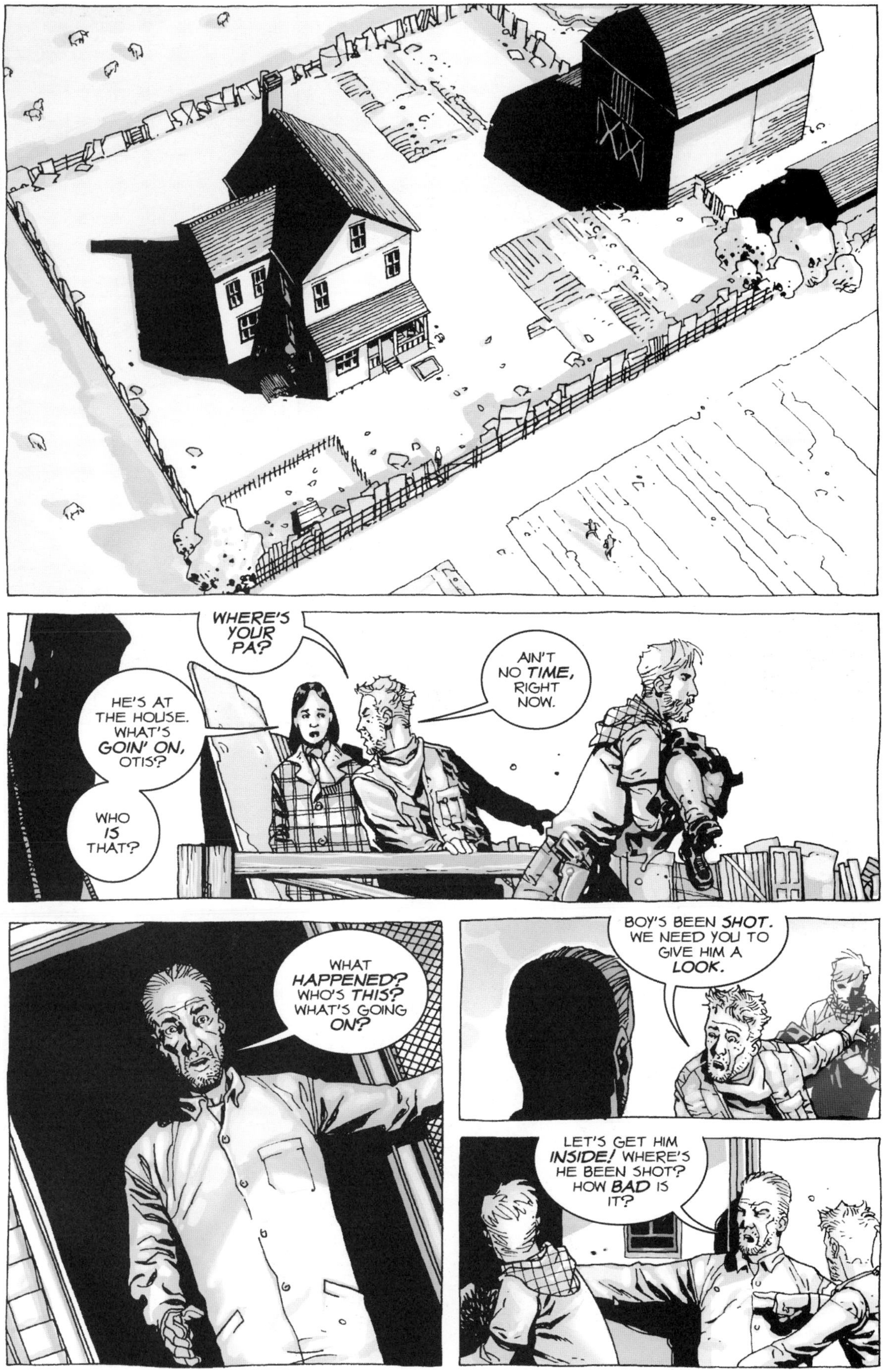
WHERE'S YOUR PA?
HE'S AT THE HOUSE. WHAT'S GOIN' ON, OTIS?
AIN'T NO TIME, RIGHT NOW.
WHO IS THAT?
WHAT HAPPENED? WHO'S THIS? WHAT'S GOING ON?
BOY'S BEEN SHOT. WE NEED YOU TO GIVE HIM A LOOK.
LET'S GET HIM INSIDE! WHERE'S HE BEEN SHOT? HOW BAD IS IT?

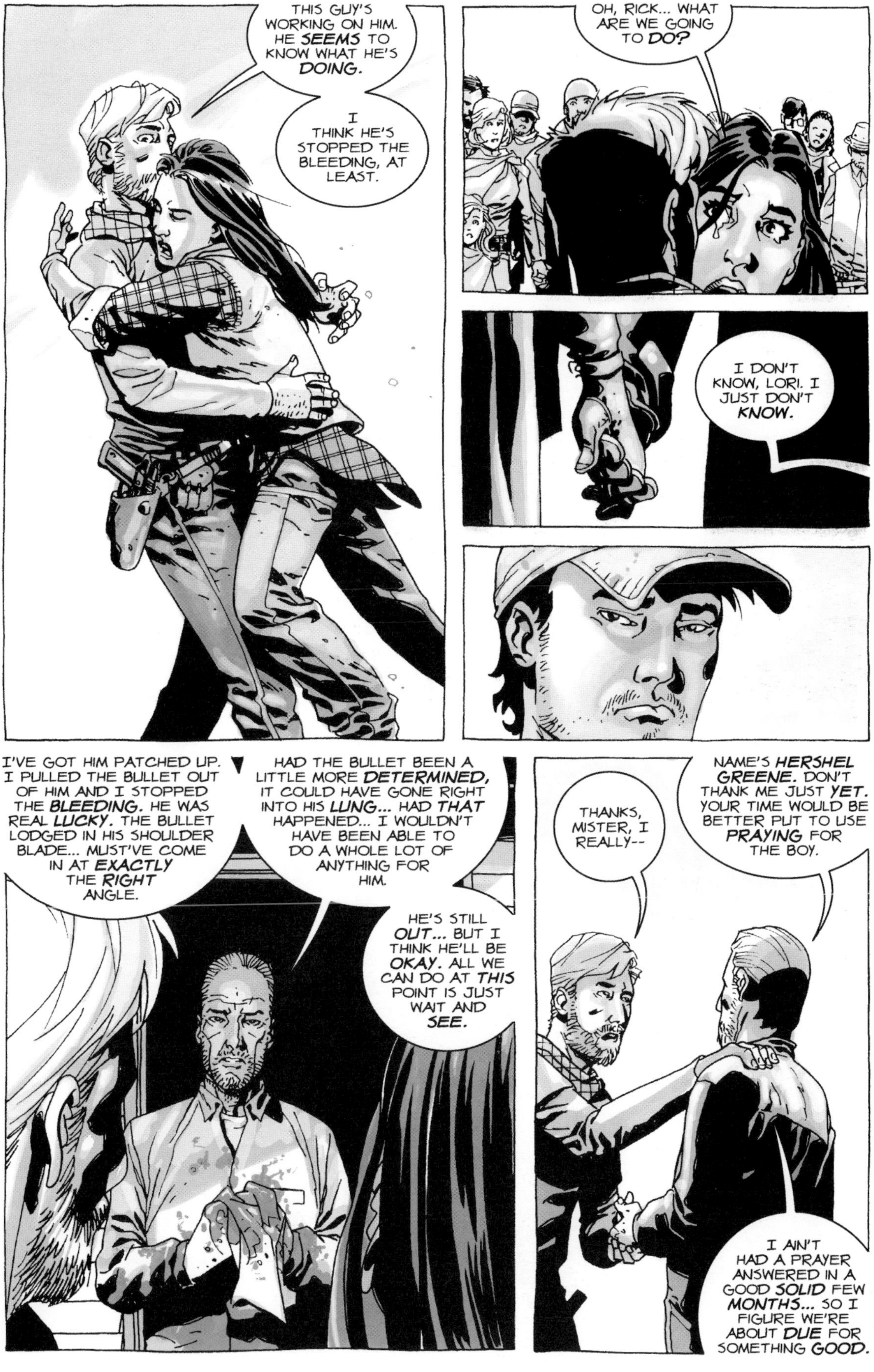

THIS GUY'S WORKING ON HIM. HE SEEMS TO KNOW WHAT HE'S DOING.
I THINK HE'S STOPPED THE BLEEDING, AT LEAST.
OH, RICK... WHAT ARE WE GOING TO DO?
I DON'T KNOW, LORI. I JUST DON'T KNOW.
I'VE GOT HIM PATCHED UP. I PULLED THE BULLET OUT OF HIM AND I STOPPED THE BLEEDING. HE WAS REAL LUCKY. THE BULLET LODGED IN HIS SHOULDER BLADE... MUST'VE COME IN AT EXACTLY THE RIGHT ANGLE.
HAD THE BULLET BEEN A LITTLE MORE DETERMINED, IT COULD HAVE GONE RIGHT INTO HIS LUNG... HAD THAT HAPPENED... I WOULDN'T HAVE BEEN ABLE TO DO A WHOLE LOT OF ANYTHING FOR HIM.
HE'S STILL OUT... BUT I THINK HE'LL BE OKAY. ALL WE CAN DO AT THIS POINT IS JUST WAIT AND SEE.
THANKS, MISTER, I REALLY--
NAME'S HERSHEL GREENE. DON'T THANK ME JUST YET. YOUR TIME WOULD BE BETTER PUT TO USE PRAYING FOR THE BOY.
I AIN'T HAD A PRAYER ANSWERED IN A GOOD SOLID FEW MONTHS... SO I FIGURE WE'RE ABOUT DUE FOR SOMETHING GOOD.

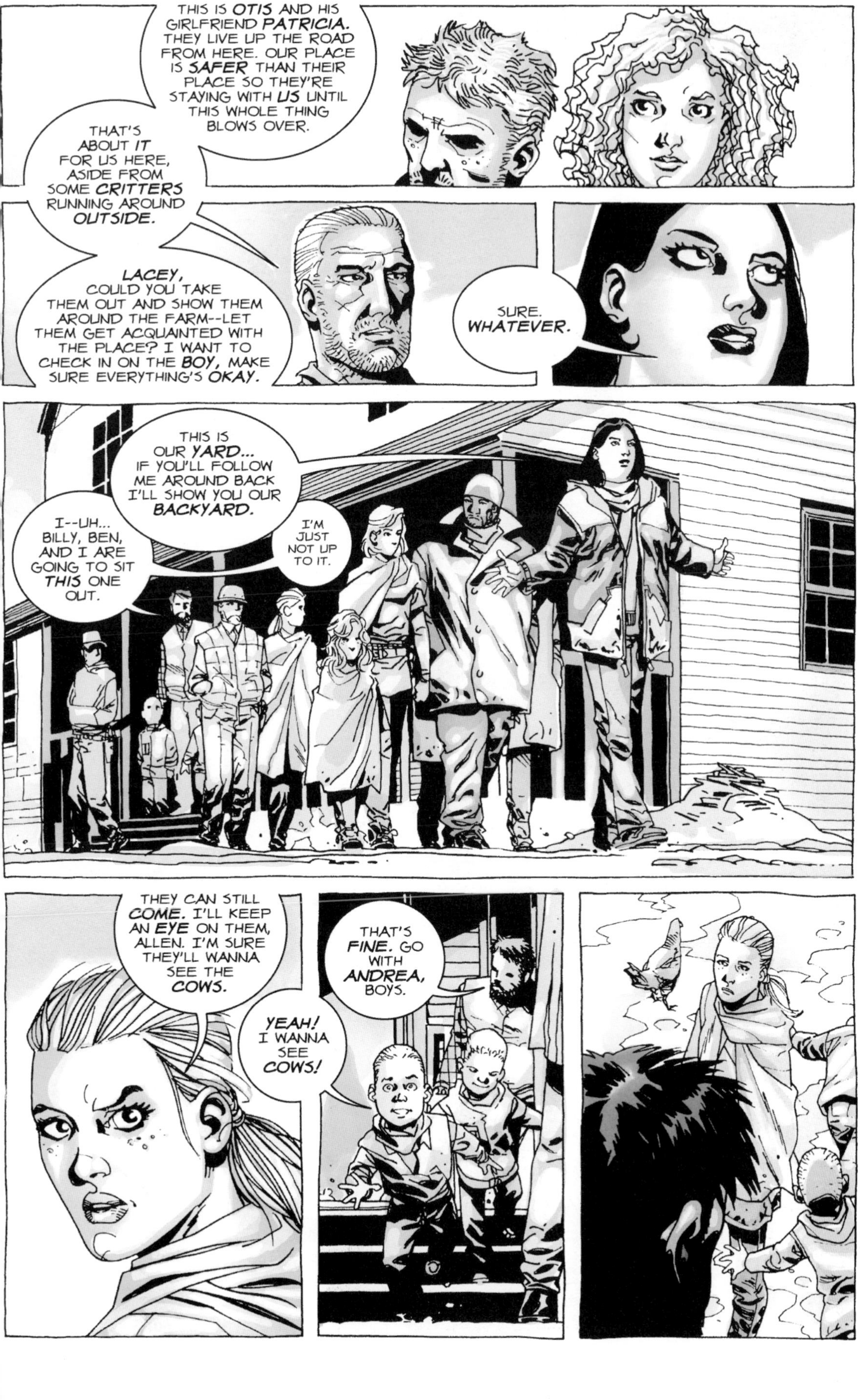
THIS IS OTIS AND HIS GIRLFRIEND PATRICIA. THEY LIVE UP THE ROAD FROM HERE. OUR PLACE IS SAFER THAN THEIR PLACE SO THEY'RE STAYING WITH US UNTIL THIS WHOLE THING BLOWS OVER.
THAT'S ABOUT IT FOR US HERE, ASIDE FROM SOME CRITTERS RUNNING AROUND OUTSIDE.
LACEY, COULD YOU TAKE THEM OUT AND SHOW THEM AROUND THE FARM--LET THEM GET ACQUAINTED WITH THE PLACE? I WANT TO CHECK IN ON THE BOY, MAKE SURE EVERYTHING'S OKAY.
SURE. WHATEVER.
THIS IS OUR YARD... IF YOU'LL FOLLOW ME AROUND BACK I'LL SHOW YOU OUR BACKYARD.
I--UH... BILLY, BEN, AND I ARE GOING TO SIT THIS ONE OUT.
I'M JUST NOT UP TO IT.
THEY CAN STILL COME. I'LL KEEP AN EYE ON THEM, ALLEN. I'M SURE THEY'LL WANNA SEE THE COWS.
THAT'S FINE. GO WITH ANDREA, BOYS.
YEAH! I WANNA SEE COWS!

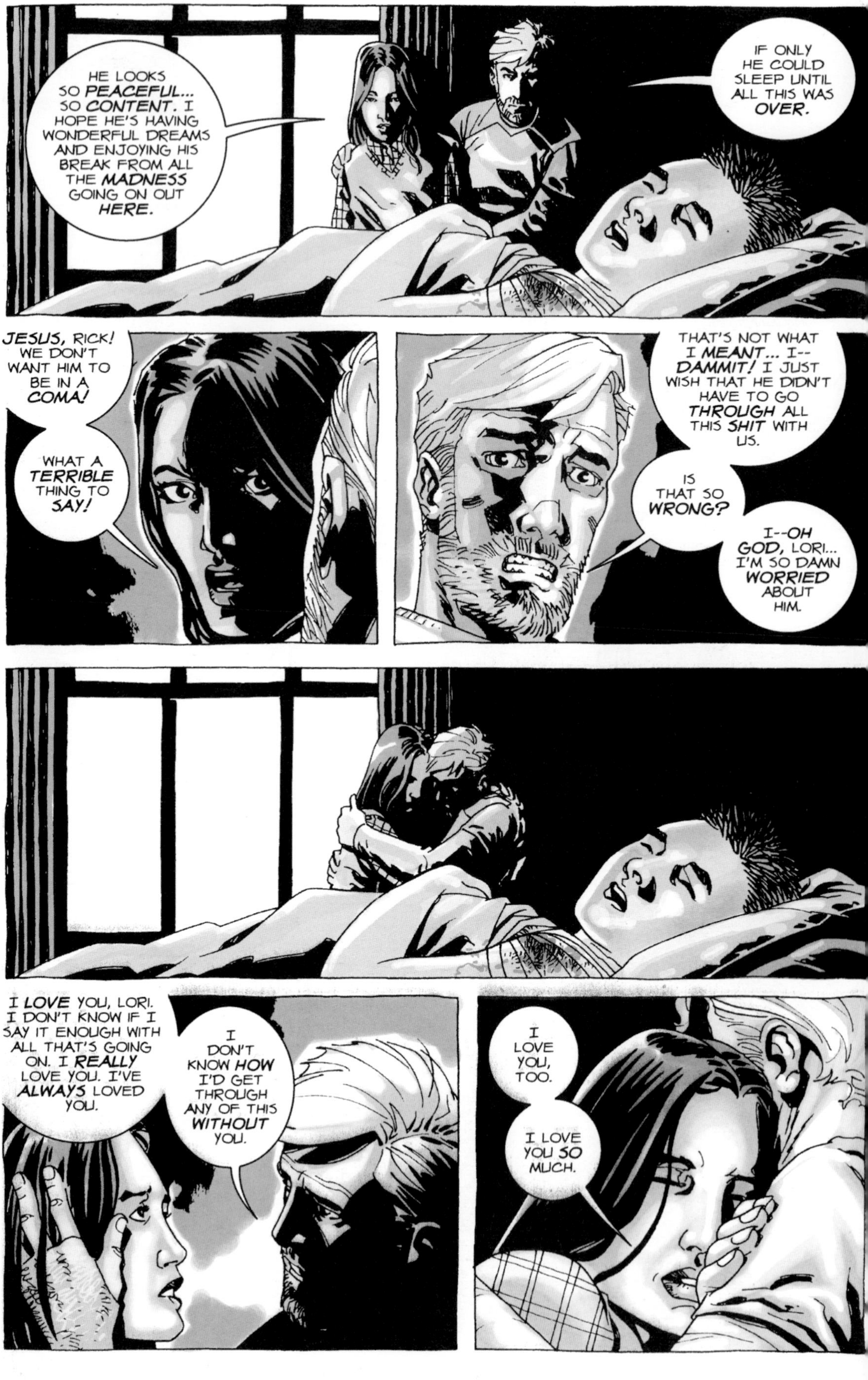
HE LOOKS SO PEACEFUL... SO CONTENT. I HOPE HE'S HAVING WONDERFUL DREAMS AND ENJOYING HIS BREAK FROM ALL THE MADNESS GOING ON OUT HERE.
IF ONLY HE COULD SLEEP UNTIL ALL THIS WAS OVER.
JESUS, RICK! WE DON'T WANT HIM TO BE IN A COMA!
WHAT A TERRIBLE THING TO SAY!
THAT'S NOT WHAT I MEANT... I-- DAMMIT! I JUST WISH THAT HE DIDN'T HAVE TO GO THROUGH ALL THIS SHIT WITH US.
IS THAT SO WRONG?
I--OH GOD, LORI... I'M SO DAMN WORRIED ABOUT HIM.
I LOVE YOU, LORI. I DON'T KNOW IF I SAY IT ENOUGH WITH ALL THAT'S GOING ON. I REALLY LOVE YOU. I'VE ALWAYS LOVED YOU.
I DON'T KNOW HOW I'D GET THROUGH ANY OF THIS WITHOUT YOU.
I LOVE YOU, TOO.
I LOVE YOU SO MUCH.

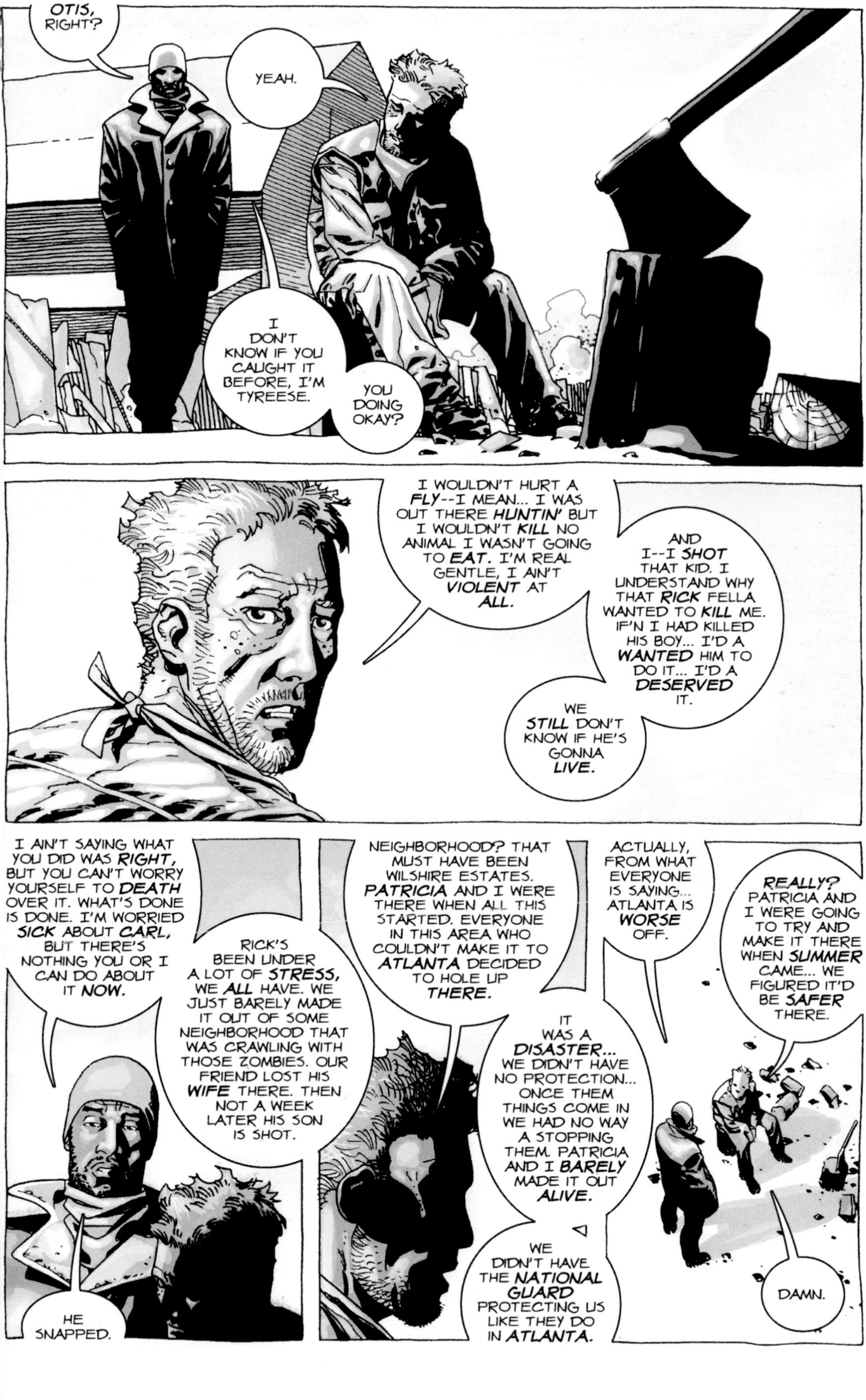
OTIS, RIGHT?
YEAH.
I DON'T KNOW IF YOU CAUGHT IT BEFORE, I'M TYREESE.
YOU DOING OKAY?
I WOULDN'T HURT A FLY--I MEAN... I WAS OUT THERE HUNTIN' BUT I WOULDN'T KILL NO ANIMAL I WASN'T GOING TO EAT. I'M REAL GENTLE, I AIN'T VIOLENT AT ALL.
AND I--I SHOT THAT KID. I UNDERSTAND WHY THAT RICK FELLA WANTED TO KILL ME. IF'N I HAD KILLED HIS BOY... I'D A WANTED HIM TO DO IT... I'D A DESERVED IT.
WE STILL DON'T KNOW IF HE'S GONNA LIVE.
I AIN'T SAYING WHAT YOU DID WAS RIGHT, BUT YOU CAN'T WORRY YOURSELF TO DEATH OVER IT. WHAT'S DONE IS DONE. I'M WORRIED SICK ABOUT CARL, BUT THERE'S NOTHING YOU OR I CAN DO ABOUT IT NOW.
RICK'S BEEN UNDER A LOT OF STRESS, WE ALL HAVE. WE JUST BARELY MADE IT OUT OF SOME NEIGHBORHOOD THAT WAS CRAWLING WITH THOSE ZOMBIES. OUR FRIEND LOST HIS WIFE THERE. THEN NOT A WEEK LATER HIS SON IS SHOT.
HE SNAPPED.
NEIGHBORHOOD? THAT MUST HAVE BEEN WILSHIRE ESTATES. PATRICIA AND I WERE THERE WHEN ALL THIS STARTED. EVERYONE IN THIS AREA WHO COULDN'T MAKE IT TO ATLANTA DECIDED TO HOLE UP THERE.
IT WAS A DISASTER... WE DIDN'T HAVE NO PROTECTION... ONCE THEM THINGS COME IN WE HAD NO WAY A STOPPING THEM. PATRICIA AND I BARELY MADE IT OUT ALIVE.
WE DIDN'T HAVE THE NATIONAL GUARD PROTECTING US LIKE THEY DO IN ATLANTA.
ACTUALLY, FROM WHAT EVERYONE IS SAYING... ATLANTA IS WORSE OFF.
REALLY? PATRICIA AND I WERE GOING TO TRY AND MAKE IT THERE WHEN SUMMER CAME... WE FIGURED IT'D BE SAFER THERE.
DAMN.

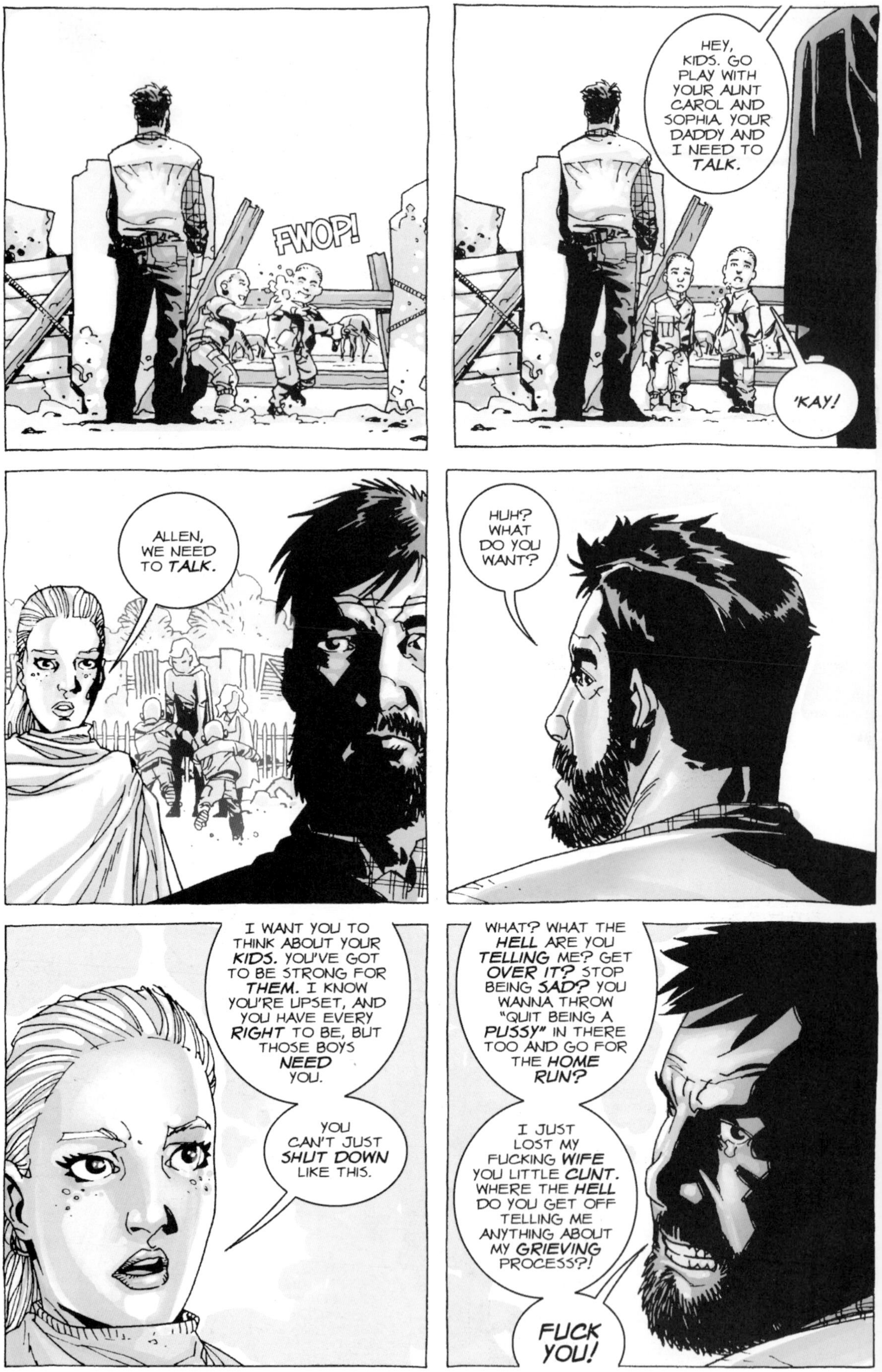
FWOP!
HEY, KIDS. GO PLAY WITH YOUR AUNT CAROL AND SOPHIA. YOUR DADDY AND I NEED TO TALK.
'KAY!
ALLEN, WE NEED TO TALK.
HUH? WHAT DO YOU WANT?
I WANT YOU TO THINK ABOUT YOUR KIDS. YOU'VE GOT TO BE STRONG FOR THEM. I KNOW YOU'RE UPSET, AND YOU HAVE EVERY RIGHT TO BE, BUT THOSE BOYS NEED YOU.
YOU CAN'T JUST SHUT DOWN LIKE THIS.
WHAT? WHAT THE HELL ARE YOU TELLING ME? GET OVER IT? STOP BEING SAD? YOU WANNA THROW "QUIT BEING A PUSSY" IN THERE TOO AND GO FOR THE HOME RUN?
I JUST LOST MY FUCKING WIFE YOU LITTLE CUNT. WHERE THE HELL DO YOU GET OFF TELLING ME ANYTHING ABOUT MY GRIEVING PROCESS?!
FUCK YOU!

WHAT? I DON'T KNOW WHAT IT'S LIKE TO **LOSE** SOMEONE?! I JUST LOST MY FUCKING **SISTER!** I THINK I KNOW A LITTLE ABOUT THE GRIEVING PROCESS. I KNOW **EXACTLY** WHAT YOU'RE GOING THROUGH! I **SHUT DOWN** WHEN I LOST AMY. I DIDN'T SPEAK FOR **DAYS**... I COULDN'T **THINK**... I ALMOST LOST MY MIND.

MY **WIFE JUST DIED!**

YOU DON'T HAVE THAT **LUXURY.** BEN AND BILLY **NEED** THEIR FATHER **RIGHT NOW!** I WAS JUST TRYING TO HELP YOU, **ASSHOLE.**

AND MY **SISTER** DIED, AND **SHANE** DIED, AND **JIM** DIED! MY **PARENTS** ARE PROBABLY DEAD! EVERYONE I'VE **EVER** KNOWN ARE PROBABLY DEAD!

MY **FRIENDS,** MY **FAMILY,** MY **NEIGHBORS,** MY **CO-WORKERS**... EVERYONE.

EVERYONE IN THIS **GROUP** IS DEALING WITH THAT... WE'RE **SURROUNDED** BY DEATH. IT'S TAKEN OVER OUR **LIVES.** AND THERE ISN'T A **GODDAMN** THING WE CAN **DO** ABOUT IT!

WE EITHER **DEAL** WITH IT OR WE **DON'T** AND RIGHT NOW YOUR SONS **NEED** YOU TO **DEAL** WITH IT... AND **GET OVER IT.**

THEY **NEED** YOU! THINK ABOUT **THEM!**

ALL I **CAN** DO IS THINK ABOUT THEM! IT'S **ALL** I'VE **DONE** NOW FOR **DAYS!** I THINK ABOUT THEM GROWING UP WITHOUT THEIR **MOTHER**... I THINK ABOUT THEM GETTING **OLDER**... **FORGETTING** ABOUT HER... NOT EVEN REMEMBERING HER **FACE.**

YOU LITTLE **BITCH.** DON'T COME OVER HERE AND TRY AND GIVE ME **ADVICE.** YOU DON'T KNOW **SHIT.** YOU'RE NOT **HELPING** ONE BIT.

I'M THINKING ABOUT **THAT** AND IT'S TEARING ME **APART!**

LEAVE ME THE **FUCK** ALONE!

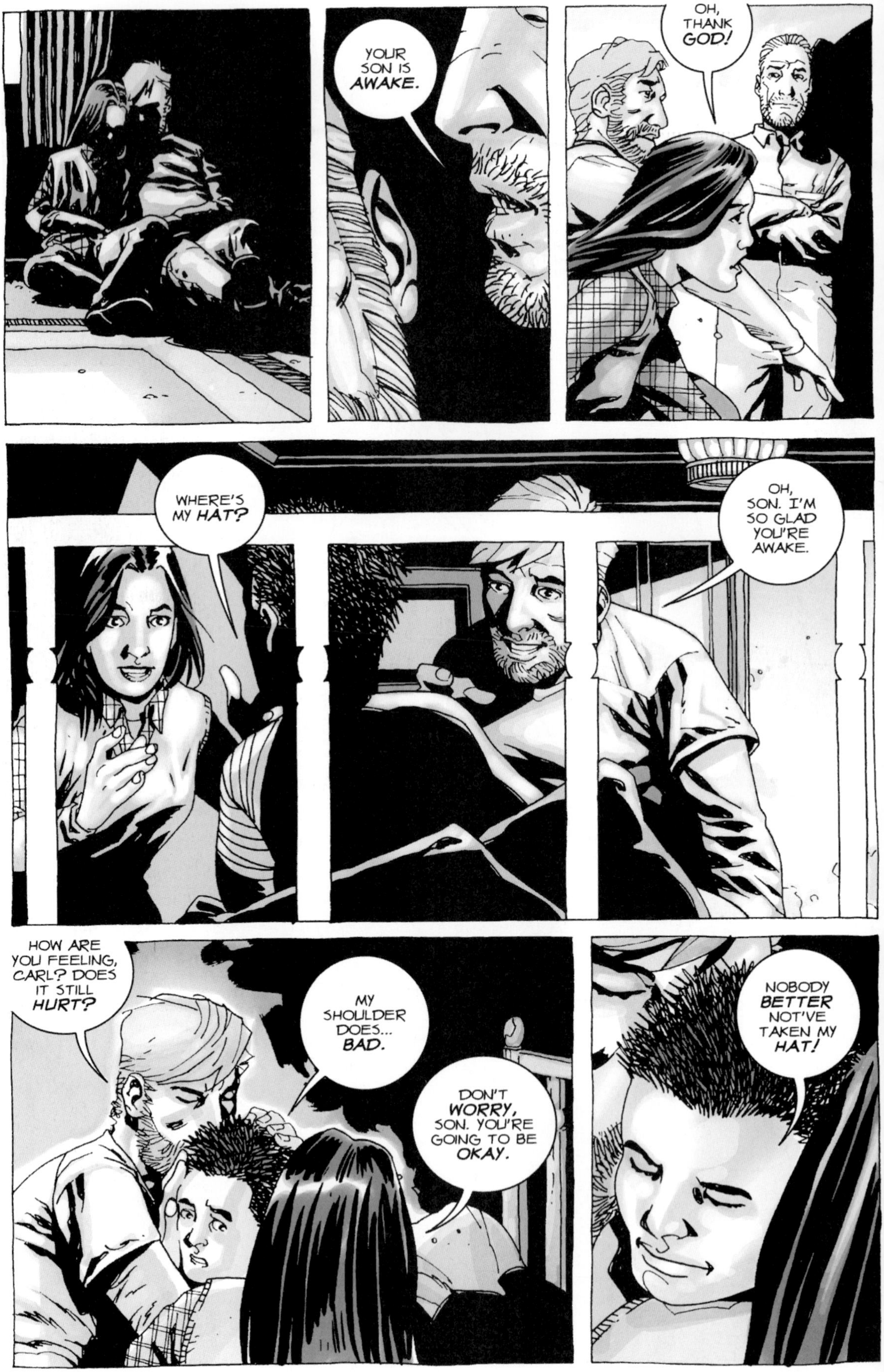
YOUR SON IS AWAKE.
OH, THANK GOD!
WHERE'S MY HAT?
OH, SON. I'M SO GLAD YOU'RE AWAKE.
HOW ARE YOU FEELING, CARL? DOES IT STILL HURT?
MY SHOULDER DOES... BAD.
DON'T WORRY, SON. YOU'RE GOING TO BE OKAY.
NOBODY BETTER NOT'VE TAKEN MY HAT!

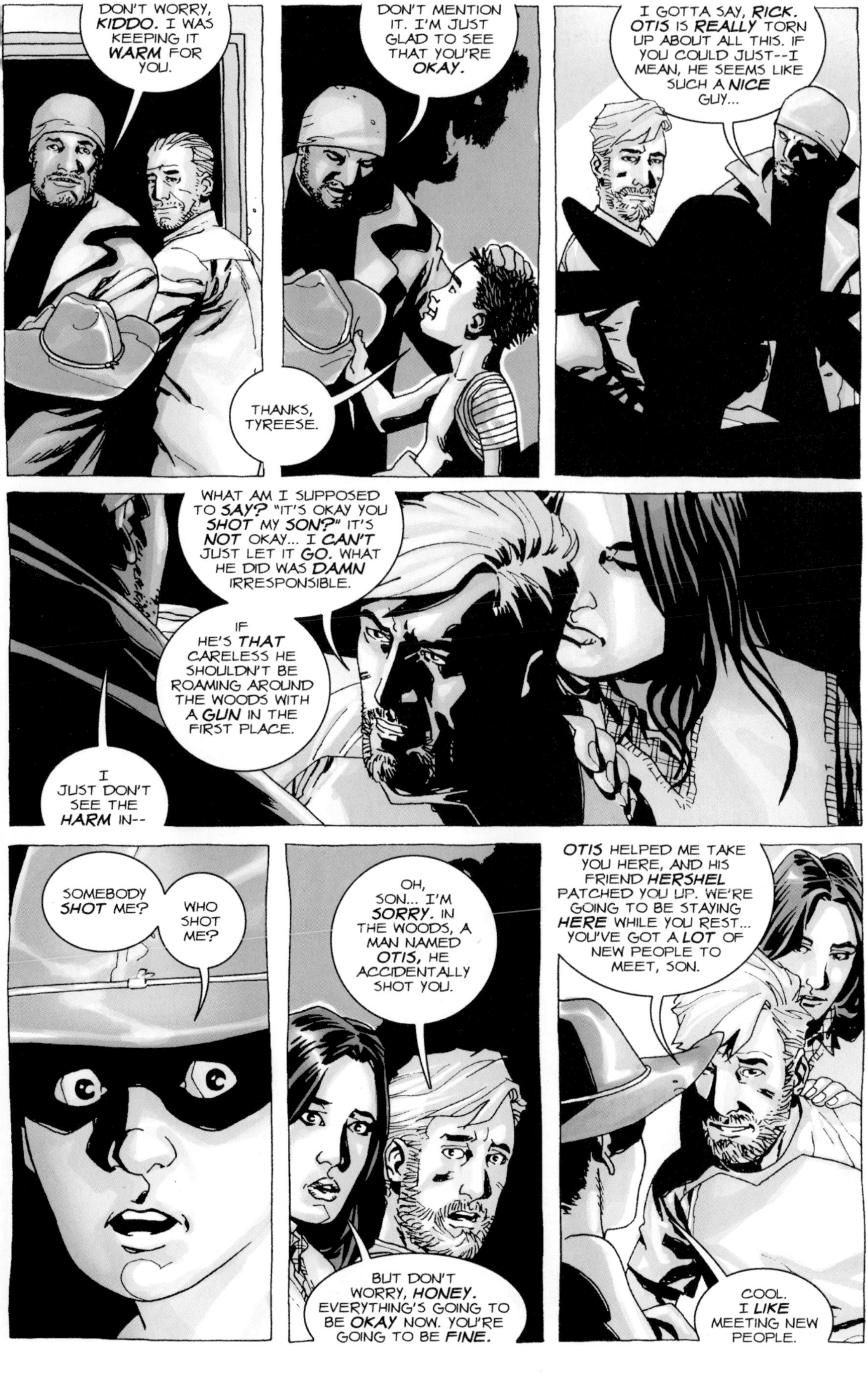
DON'T WORRY, KIDDO. I WAS KEEPING IT WARM FOR YOU.
DON'T MENTION IT. I'M JUST GLAD TO SEE THAT YOU'RE OKAY.
THANKS, TYREESE.
I GOTTA SAY, RICK. OTIS IS REALLY TORN UP ABOUT ALL THIS. IF YOU COULD JUST--I MEAN, HE SEEMS LIKE SUCH A NICE GUY...
WHAT AM I SUPPOSED TO SAY? "IT'S OKAY YOU SHOT MY SON?" IT'S NOT OKAY... I CAN'T JUST LET IT GO. WHAT HE DID WAS DAMN IRRESPONSIBLE.
IF HE'S THAT CARELESS HE SHOULDN'T BE ROAMING AROUND THE WOODS WITH A GUN IN THE FIRST PLACE.
I JUST DON'T SEE THE HARM IN--
SOMEBODY SHOT ME?
WHO SHOT ME?
OH, SON... I'M SORRY. IN THE WOODS, A MAN NAMED OTIS, HE ACCIDENTALLY SHOT YOU.
BUT DON'T WORRY, HONEY. EVERYTHING'S GOING TO BE OKAY NOW. YOU'RE GOING TO BE FINE.
OTIS HELPED ME TAKE YOU HERE, AND HIS FRIEND HERSHEL PATCHED YOU UP. WE'RE GOING TO BE STAYING HERE WHILE YOU REST... YOU'VE GOT A LOT OF NEW PEOPLE TO MEET, SON.
COOL. I LIKE MEETING NEW PEOPLE.

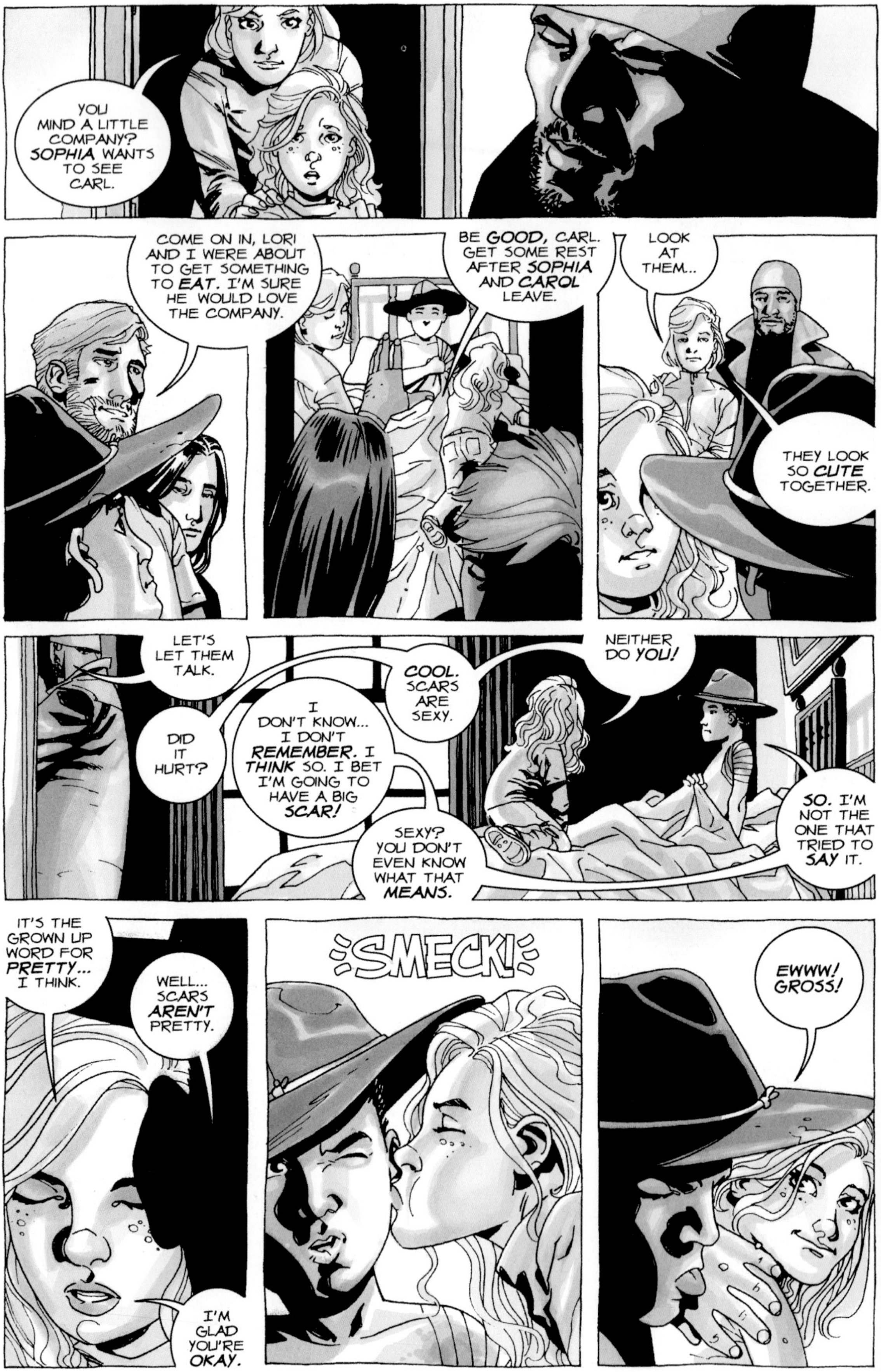

YOU MIND A LITTLE COMPANY? SOPHIA WANTS TO SEE CARL.
COME ON IN, LORI AND I WERE ABOUT TO GET SOMETHING TO EAT. I'M SURE HE WOULD LOVE THE COMPANY.
BE GOOD, CARL. GET SOME REST AFTER SOPHIA AND CAROL LEAVE.
LOOK AT THEM...
THEY LOOK SO CUTE TOGETHER.
LET'S LET THEM TALK.
DID IT HURT?
I DON'T KNOW... I DON'T REMEMBER. I THINK SO. I BET I'M GOING TO HAVE A BIG SCAR!
COOL. SCARS ARE SEXY.
SEXY? YOU DON'T EVEN KNOW WHAT THAT MEANS.
NEITHER DO YOU!
SO. I'M NOT THE ONE THAT TRIED TO SAY IT.
IT'S THE GROWN UP WORD FOR PRETTY... I THINK.
WELL... SCARS AREN'T PRETTY.
I'M GLAD YOU'RE OKAY.
SMECK!
EWWW! GROSS!

LORI?

WHAT CAN I **DO** FOR YOU, DALE?

I'M GOING TO **TALK**, AND YOU'RE GOING TO **LISTEN**. I'M AN OLD MAN... TOO OLD FOR **ARGUMENTS**. SO I WANT YOU TO KNOW THAT I REALLY DON'T WANT THIS TO BECOME ONE. I'M GOING TO **SAY** WHAT I HAVE TO **SAY** AND THEN WE'RE **DONE**.

RICK IS THE **BACKBONE** OF THIS GROUP. HE'S THE **ONE** STABLE THING WE'VE **ALL** GOT. HE **KNOWS** THIS. THAT'S WHY WHEN HE'S SCARED YOU **CAN'T TELL**... YOU **KNOW** HE'S SCARED, BUT HE AIN'T SHOWING IT. WE **NEED** THAT. WE NEED **HIM**.

I DON'T KNOW **WHAT** YOU DID WITH **SHANE**. I DON'T KNOW WHAT YOU DID TO PUT **IDEAS** IN HIS **HEAD**, BUT IF THAT BABY'S HIS... AND **NOT** RICK'S, I'M **BEGGING** YOU--TAKE IT TO YOUR **GRAVE**.

IT'LL **KILL** HIM. IT'LL BE THE ONE LAST THING IT TAKES TO MAKE HIM **CRACK**. AND WE **DON'T** NEED THAT.

I'M NOT **ACCUSING** YOU OF **SHIT** SO DON'T TRY TO **DEFEND** YOURSELF. I JUST WANTED TO SAY MY PIECE AND I APPRECIATE YOU SITTING THROUGH IT.

I THINK THEY'RE DONE WITH **DINNER**. LET'S GO EAT.

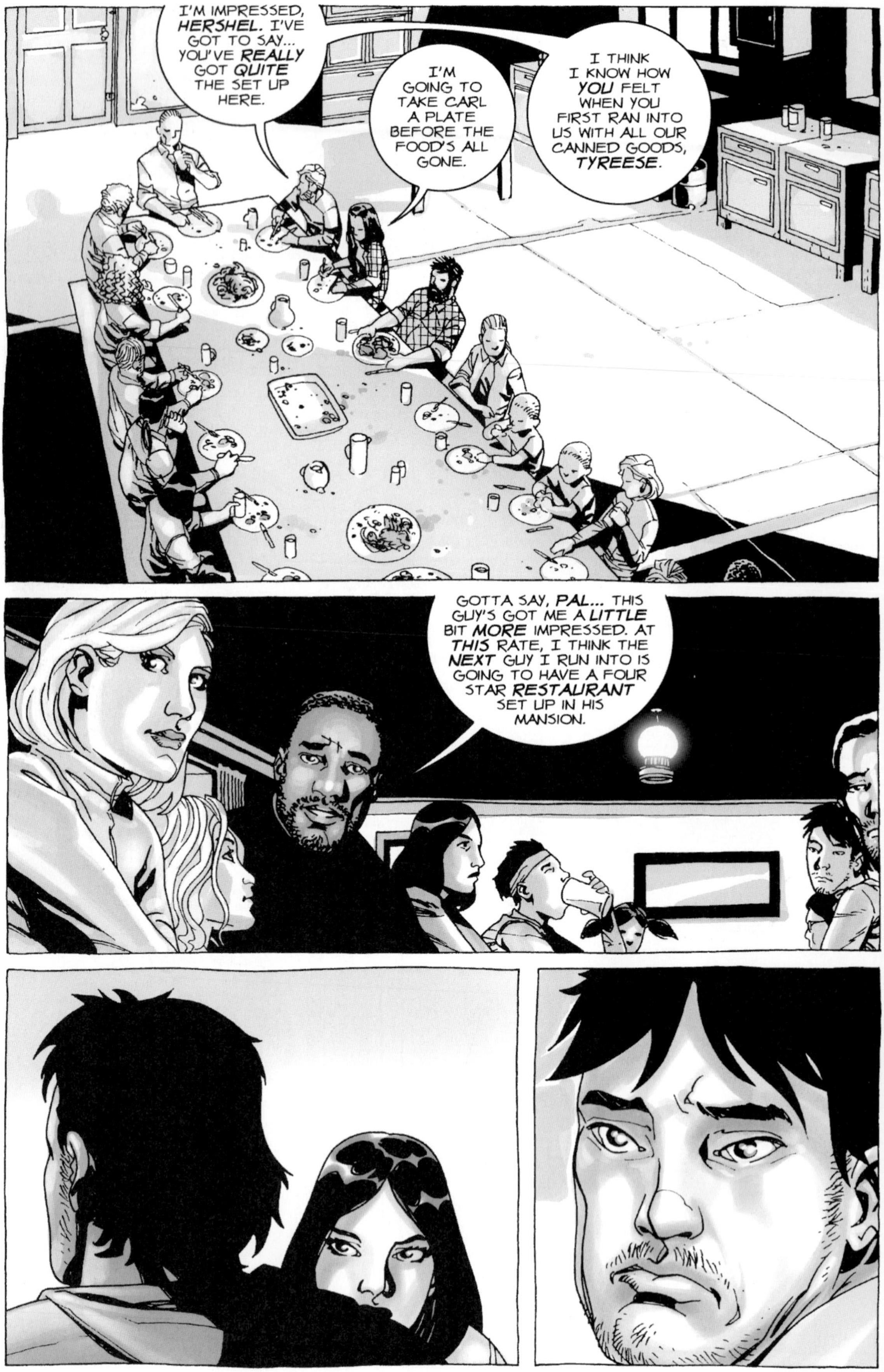
I'M IMPRESSED, HERSHEL. I'VE GOT TO SAY... YOU'VE REALLY GOT QUITE THE SET UP HERE.
I'M GOING TO TAKE CARL A PLATE BEFORE THE FOOD'S ALL GONE.
I THINK I KNOW HOW YOU FELT WHEN YOU FIRST RAN INTO US WITH ALL OUR CANNED GOODS, TYREESE.
GOTTA SAY, PAL... THIS GUY'S GOT ME A LITTLE BIT MORE IMPRESSED. AT THIS RATE, I THINK THE NEXT GUY I RUN INTO IS GOING TO HAVE A FOUR STAR RESTAURANT SET UP IN HIS MANSION.

MY **DAD** OWNED THIS PLACE. I **GREW UP** ON THIS FARM. BUT I **NEVER** LIKED IT. I WANTED TO BE A VETERINARIAN... SO THAT'S WHAT I DID. WORKING ON CREATURES GREAT AND SMALL WAS MY CALLING... AND I DID IT FOR **YEARS.**

AFTER MY **WIFE** DIED MY PRACTICE FELL APART... **SHE** ALWAYS HELD UP THE BUSINESS END... ALL I DID WAS WORK ON THE ANIMALS.

I COULDN'T DO MUCH OF **ANYTHING** WITHOUT **HER.**

SORRY TO HEAR ABOUT THAT. HOW LONG AGO WAS IT?

SHE PASSED ON ALMOST **SIX YEARS** AGO. IT WAS MY FATHER'S DYING WISH THAT I WOULD COME BACK AND WORK ON THE **FARM.**

IT JUST **SEEMED** LIKE THE RIGHT THING TO DO.

I'VE BEEN AT IT FOR FIVE YEARS NOW. IT'S **HONEST** WORK, I CAN SEE WHY MY DAD LOVED IT SO MUCH. THERE'S NOTHING QUITE LIKE LIVING OFF THE **LAND**... PROVIDING FOR **YOURSELF**... KNOWING **EXACTLY** WHERE **EVERY** PIECE OF FOOD YOU **EAT** COMES FROM.

IT'S CERTAINLY COME IN HANDY IN LIGHT OF CURRENT EVENTS.

THAT'S FOR **SURE.** SEEMS LIKE YOU'VE GOT A NICE, **STABLE** SET UP HERE.

YOU'RE WELCOME TO ENJOY IT WHILE *CARL* HEALS. I'D *RECOMMEND* STAYING HERE IN THAT TIME. IT WOULDN'T BE GOOD FOR HIM TO BE OUT IN THE *ELEMENTS* AGAIN... AT LEAST NOT *RIGHT* AWAY.

WE DON'T HAVE MUCH ROOM IN THE HOUSE, YOU'D STILL HAVE TO SLEEP IN YOUR *RV*, BUT WE GOT *PLENTY* OF FOOD AND DURING THE DAY YOU WON'T HAVE TO WORRY ABOUT BEING *SAFE*.

WHAT ABOUT YOUR *BARN?* YOU THINK WE COULD MOVE INTO THAT PLACE? MOST OF US ARE PRETTY *SICK* OF CRAMMING INTO THAT *RV*.

THE *BARN?* YOU DON'T WANT TO GO IN THERE, *TRUST ME*.

THAT'S WHERE WE KEEP ALL OUR DEAD ONES.

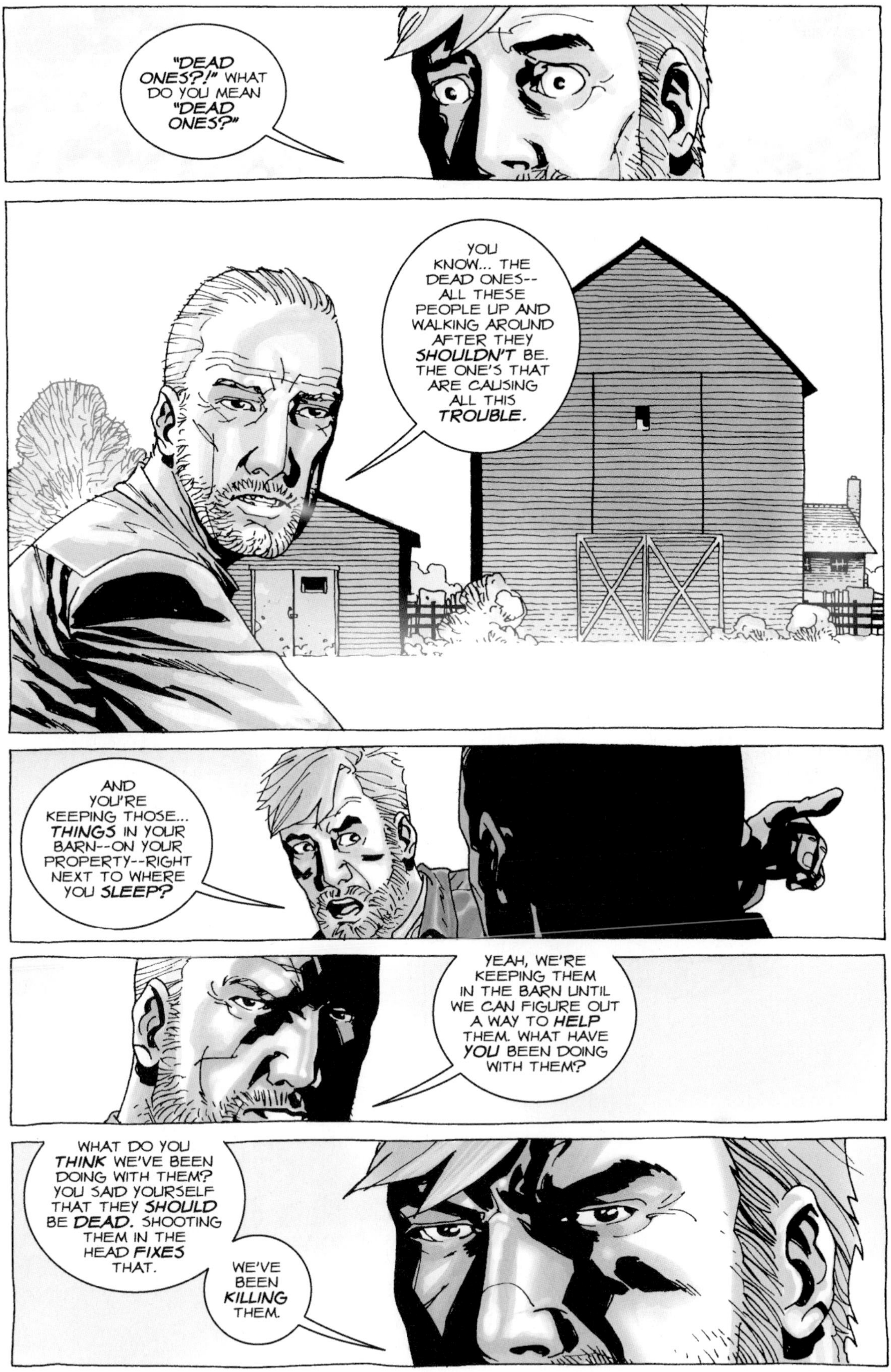
"DEAD ONES?!" WHAT DO YOU MEAN "DEAD ONES?"
YOU KNOW... THE DEAD ONES-- ALL THESE PEOPLE UP AND WALKING AROUND AFTER THEY SHOULDN'T BE. THE ONE'S THAT ARE CAUSING ALL THIS TROUBLE.
AND YOU'RE KEEPING THOSE... THINGS IN YOUR BARN--ON YOUR PROPERTY--RIGHT NEXT TO WHERE YOU SLEEP?
YEAH, WE'RE KEEPING THEM IN THE BARN UNTIL WE CAN FIGURE OUT A WAY TO HELP THEM. WHAT HAVE YOU BEEN DOING WITH THEM?
WHAT DO YOU THINK WE'VE BEEN DOING WITH THEM? YOU SAID YOURSELF THAT THEY SHOULD BE DEAD. SHOOTING THEM IN THE HEAD FIXES THAT.
WE'VE BEEN KILLING THEM.

WE'RE PUTTING THEM OUT OF THEIR *MISERY*, AND KEEPING THEM FROM *KILLING* US! THOSE THINGS *AREN'T* HUMAN. THEY'RE UNDEAD *MONSTERS*.

THEY'RE TRYING TO *EAT* US FOR GOD'S SAKE!

KILLING THEM?! YOU'VE JUST BEEN *KILLING* THEM?!

YOU DON'T KNOW *WHY!* YOU DON'T EVEN KNOW WHAT'S *WRONG* WITH THEM. *NOBODY* DOES. WE DON'T KNOW A *DAMN* THING ABOUT WHAT HAPPENED OR WHAT'S GOING ON.

I KNOW THOSE THINGS ARE TRYING TO *KILL* US--AND THAT THE LESS OF *THEM* THERE ARE OUT THERE THE SAFER *WE'LL* BE! AND I KNOW IT'S NOT *SMART* TO HAVE A MESS OF THEM PINNED UP NOT *THIRTY FEET* FROM YOUR *GODDAMN* HOUSE!

WE SHOULD GO IN THAT BARN RIGHT NOW AND *SHOOT* EVERY *GODDAMN* ONE OF THEM IN THE HEAD. IT'S NOT *SAFE* FOR THEM TO BE HERE! WE NEED TO KILL *THEM* BEFORE THEY KILL *US!*

MY *SON* IS IN THERE, *GOD DAMMIT!*

YOUR *SON?*

SHAWN WAS *BITTEN.* IT WAS BEFORE WE PUT UP THE BARRIER AROUND THE HOUSE. I--I COULDN'T HELP HIM, HE DIED AFTER A COUPLE DAYS... AND TURNED INTO ONE OF *THEM.*

I DIDN'T KNOW WHAT *ELSE* TO *DO.* SO I KEPT SHAWN IN THE BARN. HE TRIED TO ATTACK US... TO--*KILL* US. BUT I COULDN'T KILL HIM... I COULDN'T BRING MYSELF TO DO *THAT.* WHEN WE FOUND OTHERS... WE JUST... WE KEPT *THEM* TOO.

HERSHEL, I-- I'M REALLY *SORRY.* I *TRULY* AM. I CAN'T *IMAGINE* WHAT YOU'VE BEEN GOING THROUGH. IF I HAD LOST CARL-- I DON'T--I DON'T KNOW *WHAT* I WOULD HAVE DONE.

I DON'T THINK I COULD *LIVE* WITHOUT MY SON... BUT YOU'VE GOT TO LISTEN TO ME, *HERSHEL.* THAT THING IN THE BARN... IT'S *NOT YOUR* SON.

GET YOUR *FUCKING* HAND OFF ME!

THAP!

NOT MY SON?! WHAT MADE *YOU* SUCH A *GODDAMN EXPERT?!* I DON'T KNOW ABOUT *YOU* BUT THE ZOMBIES AROUND *HERE* DIDN'T COME WITH A FUCKING *INSTRUCTION MANUAL!*

WE DON'T KNOW A *GODDAMN THING* ABOUT THEM. WE DON'T KNOW WHAT THEY'RE *THINKING*--WHAT THEY'RE *FEELING.* WE DON'T KNOW IF IT'S A *DISEASE* OR SIDE EFFECTS OF SOME KIND OF CHEMICAL WARFARE! WE DON'T KNOW *SHIT!*

FOR ALL *WE* KNOW THESE THINGS COULD WAKE UP *TOMORROW,* HEAL UP, AND BE COMPLETELY *NORMAL* AGAIN!

WE JUST DON'T *KNOW!* YOU COULD HAVE BEEN *MURDERING* ALL THOSE PEOPLE YOU "PUT OUT OF THEIR MISERY."

THEY'RE *DEAD.* BEFORE THEY GET BACK UP--BEFORE THEY TRY TO *EAT* YOU-- THEY *DIE.* YOU SAID YOU SAW YOUR SON *DIE.* HE'S *DEAD.* THOSE THINGS ARE ROTTING *CORPSES* WITH *PIECES* MISSING... THEY'RE *NOT* SICK PEOPLE... THEY'RE *DEAD.*

RICK, *LISTEN.* THESE THINGS COULD BE IN THE EARLY STAGES OF *RECOVERY.* THEY COULD BE *HEALING...* AND THAT'S WHY THINGS AREN'T WORKING RIGHT. THIS IS ALL COMPLETELY *UNKNOWN* TO US. WE'VE GOT NO CLUE HOW TO HANDLE THIS.

I DON'T WANT TO HAVE *BLOOD* ON MY HANDS IF WE FIND OUT THESE PEOPLE *ARE* ALIVE.

NO. THEY'RE *DEAD!* I'VE SEEN THOSE THINGS WITH THEIR DAMN *GUTS* HANGING OUT. WHAT YOU'RE SAYING DOESN'T MAKE A *DAMN* BIT OF SENSE.

RICK! WE'RE *GUESTS* HERE, MAN. *WE* AREN'T MAKING THE RULES.

JUST *STOP* THIS.

YOU'RE RIGHT, *TYREESE.* SORRY.

HOW *MANY* DO YOU *HAVE* IN THERE?

FOURTEEN. WE HAD TO RAID NEARBY HOUSES FOR SUPPLIES... BLANKETS, KEROSENE, AND WHAT NOT. ALL OUR NEIGHBORS HAD TURNED. IT'S MOSTLY THEM AND THEIR KIDS... AND A COUPLE WHO HAD WANDERED ONTO THE PROPERTY.

THEY CAN'T GET OUT OF THE BARN. WE'VE GOT THEM LOCKED UP *TIGHT.* WE'RE *COMPLETELY* SAFE HERE. YOU DON'T HAVE TO WORRY.

IF YOU SAY SO. I'M *TRUSTING* YOU ON THIS ONE.

I HOPE YOU'RE RIGHT.

...

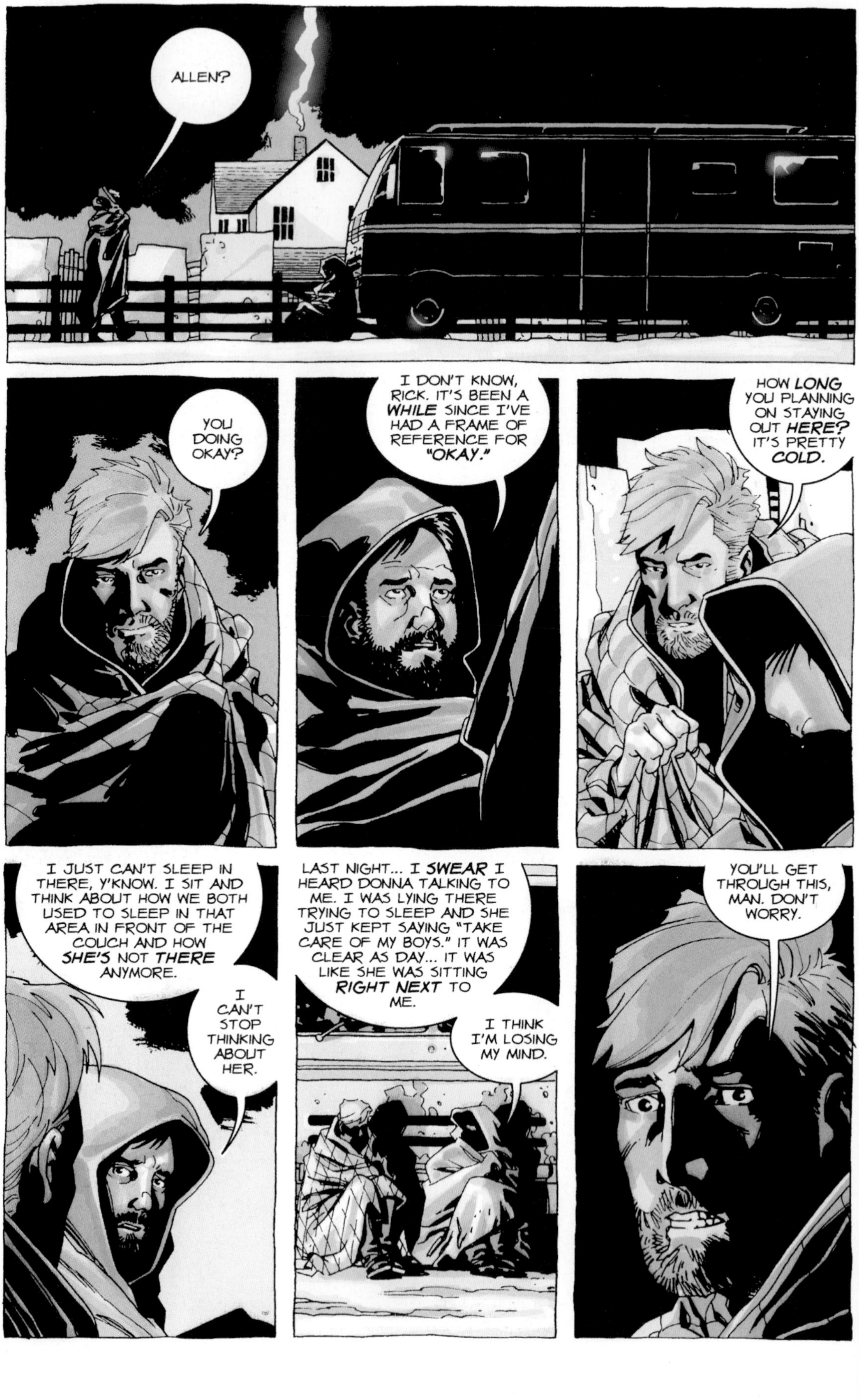
ALLEN?
YOU DOING OKAY?
I DON'T KNOW, RICK. IT'S BEEN A WHILE SINCE I'VE HAD A FRAME OF REFERENCE FOR "OKAY."
HOW LONG YOU PLANNING ON STAYING OUT HERE? IT'S PRETTY COLD.
I JUST CAN'T SLEEP IN THERE, Y'KNOW. I SIT AND THINK ABOUT HOW WE BOTH USED TO SLEEP IN THAT AREA IN FRONT OF THE COUCH AND HOW SHE'S NOT THERE ANYMORE.
I CAN'T STOP THINKING ABOUT HER.
LAST NIGHT... I SWEAR I HEARD DONNA TALKING TO ME. I WAS LYING THERE TRYING TO SLEEP AND SHE JUST KEPT SAYING "TAKE CARE OF MY BOYS." IT WAS CLEAR AS DAY... IT WAS LIKE SHE WAS SITTING RIGHT NEXT TO ME.
I THINK I'M LOSING MY MIND.
YOU'LL GET THROUGH THIS, MAN. DON'T WORRY.

MORNING, HERSHEL.

OH, *HEY.* GOOD MORNING, YOURSELF.

DID YOUR CREW SLEEP OKAY LAST NIGHT?

YEAH, THEY HAD A LITTLE EXTRA ROOM IN THE RV SINCE *LORI* AND I STAYED WITH *CARL* IN YOUR HOUSE LAST NIGHT.

THEY GOT AS MUCH SLEEP AS *EVER,* I MEAN. WE DON'T GET MUCH SLEEP ANY MORE, *ANY* OF US.

I KNOW WHAT YOU MEAN. I HAVEN'T HAD A GOOD NIGHT'S SLEEP IN *QUITE* SOME TIME.

I CAN'T IMAGINE *HOW* YOU PEOPLE MADE IT OUT AT THAT CAMP OF YOURS. I FEEL INSECURE *ENOUGH* SLEEPING IN MY *HOUSE.*

LISTEN, MAN... I WANTED TO APOLOGIZE FOR LAST NIGHT. I REALLY DIDN'T MEAN TO JUMP YOUR SHIT LIKE THAT. I'VE BEEN A LITTLE ON EDGE SINCE CARL GOT SHOT AND I WAS *WAY* OUT OF LINE.

I UNDERSTAND. WE'RE *ALL* A LITTLE ON EDGE, IT'S ONLY *NATURAL,* I DIDN'T TAKE OFFENSE.

STILL, I JUST WANTED TO LET YOU KNOW THAT I REALLY *DO* APPRECIATE ALL YOU'VE DONE FOR *CARL,* AND YOU ALLOWING US TO *STAY* HERE.

HEY, ALLEN.

CAN'T YOU TAKE A *HINT?* I HAVE *NOTHING* TO SAY TO YOU. YOU WANT TO RUN YOUR MOUTH AND GIVE PEOPLE ADVICE ON THINGS YOU *OBVIOUSLY* DON'T KNOW SHIT ABOUT... GO DO IT SOMEWHERE ELSE.

NOW HOLD ON JUST A DAMN--

I'M *SORRY,* ALLEN. I DIDN'T MEAN TO PISS YOU OFF.

NO, DALE. IT'S *OKAY.* LET IT GO.

YOU COULD HAVE *FOOLED* ME.

SOPHIA'S IN THERE TALKING WITH CARL *AGAIN*. I SWEAR... A FEW MORE YEARS AND WE'RE GOING TO HAVE TO KEEP AN *EYE* ON THOSE TWO. THEY'RE GETTING ALONG A LITTLE *TOO* WELL FOR THEIR AGE.

HEY, WHERE'D YOU GET *THAT?*

OH, THE *BOOK?* HERSHEL'S OLDEST DAUGHTER, LACEY HAS *QUITE* THE COLLECTION. I DIDN'T REALIZE HOW MUCH I *MISSED* READING. IT'S FUNNY HOW WE DON'T REALLY REALIZE THE THINGS WE'RE MISSING.

SPEAK FOR YOURSELF... I'D *KILL* FOR A VIKINGS GAME AND I'VE BEEN THINKING ABOUT THAT NONSTOP FOR *WEEKS*.

I HEAR YOU. I'D LOVE TO KNOW HOW THE RAIDERS ARE DOING. IF THERE'S *ANY* TEAM THAT COULD SURVIVE THIS... IT'S *THEM*.

HEY, LISTEN... *CHRIS* AND *JULIE* ARE GOING TO BE SHOOTING WITH US LATER TODAY, *RIGHT?* ARE THEY GOING TO BE CARRYING THEIR GUNS AT ALL TIMES?

I DON'T KNOW, *MAN*. I WANT THEM TO *BE* SAFE AND *FEEL* SAFE BUT I DON'T THINK THEY'RE *READY* TO HAVE GUNS ON THEM AT ALL TIMES. MAYBE AFTER A FEW PRACTICE SESSIONS ONCE I THINK THEY'VE GOT A GOOD HANDLE ON THINGS... BUT I'M NOT EVEN SURE I'LL BE COMFORTABLE WITH IT *THEN*.

THEY'RE *TEENAGERS*... I DON'T KNOW *WHAT'S* GOING THROUGH THEIR HEADS.

READING YOU *LOUD* AND *CLEAR*. SEE WHAT WE'VE GOT TO LOOK FORWARD TO, CAROL?

NOT *ME*. I'VE TALKED IT OVER WITH *SOPHIA* AND SHE'S SKIPPING RIGHT OVER TO HER EARLY TWENTIES.

YOU ABOUT **READY?** I'M GIVING YOU GUYS SOME LOW CALIBER GUNS SO THEY'LL BE A LITTLE **EASIER** TO HANDLE.

LET'S DO IT!

YEAH. THIS'LL BE **FUN!**

PKOW!

THIS ISN'T A **GAME,** JULIE. THIS IS SERIOUS STUFF. YOU LISTEN TO **RICK** AND DO **EVERYTHING** HE SAYS.

SHE **KNOWS,** MAN. YOU DON'T HAVE TO WORRY. WE'RE TAKING THIS SERIOUSLY.

GOOD TO KNOW. **THANKS,** CHRIS.

PTANG!

NICE ONE, MAN.

THANKS, BUT MY **TEACHER** DESERVES ALL THE CREDIT.

WHOA, WHOA! STOP SHOOTING!! STOP RIGHT NOW!

WHAT'S THE PROBLEM, HERSHEL?

THE THOMPSON'S HOUSE IS JUST ON THE OTHER SIDE OF THAT TREE LINE!

YOUR BULLETS ARE PROBABLY *RIPPING* RIGHT THROUGH THEIR *HOUSE!*

YOU *CAN'T* KEEP *FIRING* IN THAT DIRECTION!

JEEZ, *SORRY* ABOUT THAT. I HAD NO IDEA. THE *THOMPSON'S* HUH? THEY, UH...

ARE THEY IN YOUR *BARN?*

THAT'S NOT THE POINT! I DON'T WANT THEIR HOUSE TO BE *DESTROYED.* YOU CAN'T JUST--

THAT'S *NOT* WHAT I MEANT. I DIDN'T--

WHAT? WHAT'S GOING ON?

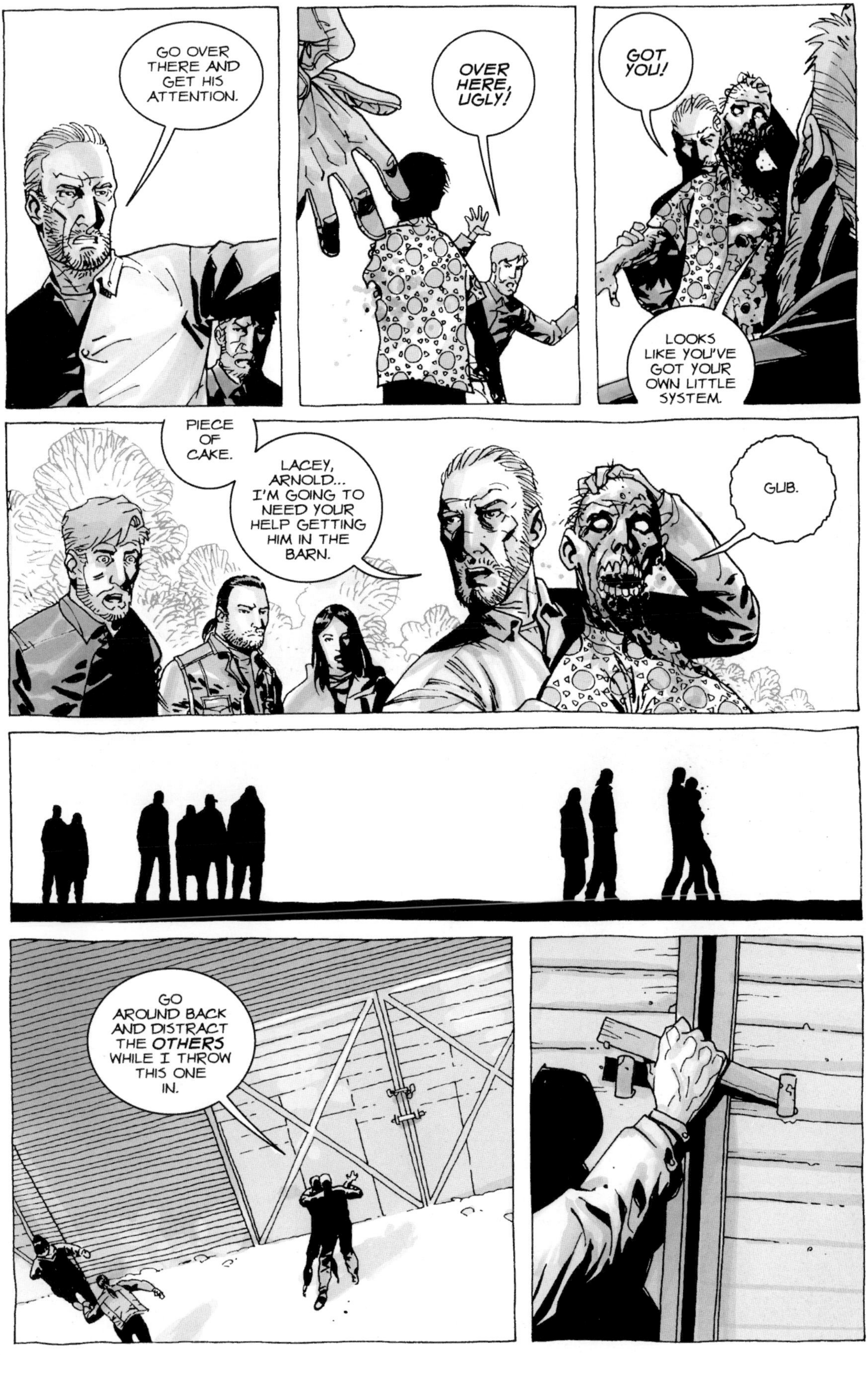
GO OVER THERE AND GET HIS ATTENTION.
OVER HERE, UGLY!
GOT YOU!
LOOKS LIKE YOU'VE GOT YOUR OWN LITTLE SYSTEM.
PIECE OF CAKE.
LACEY, ARNOLD... I'M GOING TO NEED YOUR HELP GETTING HIM IN THE BARN.
GUB.
GO AROUND BACK AND DISTRACT THE OTHERS WHILE I THROW THIS ONE IN.

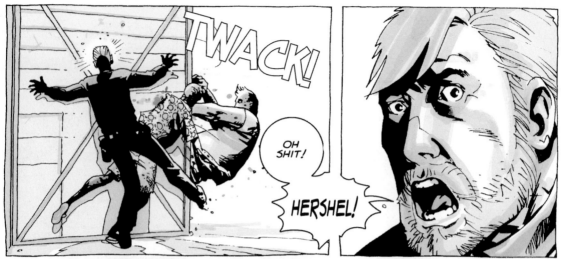

TWACK!

OH SHIT!

HERSHEL!

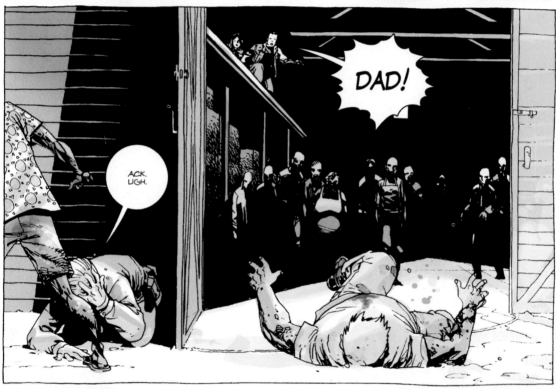

DAD!

ACK. UGH.

I'M COMING DAD!!

RUNGH!

OH GOD! OH, *PLEASE* GOD!

NO!

WHUMP!

LORI! MAKE SURE ALL THE KIDS ARE IN THE HOUSE AND *KEEP* THEM THERE!

STAY INSIDE!

NO!

CHRIS! JULIE! INTO THE HOUSE WITH LORI!

NOT MY FATHER!

NOT MY FATHER!

HUNGH.

GRAR!

AAAGG!

ARNOLD!

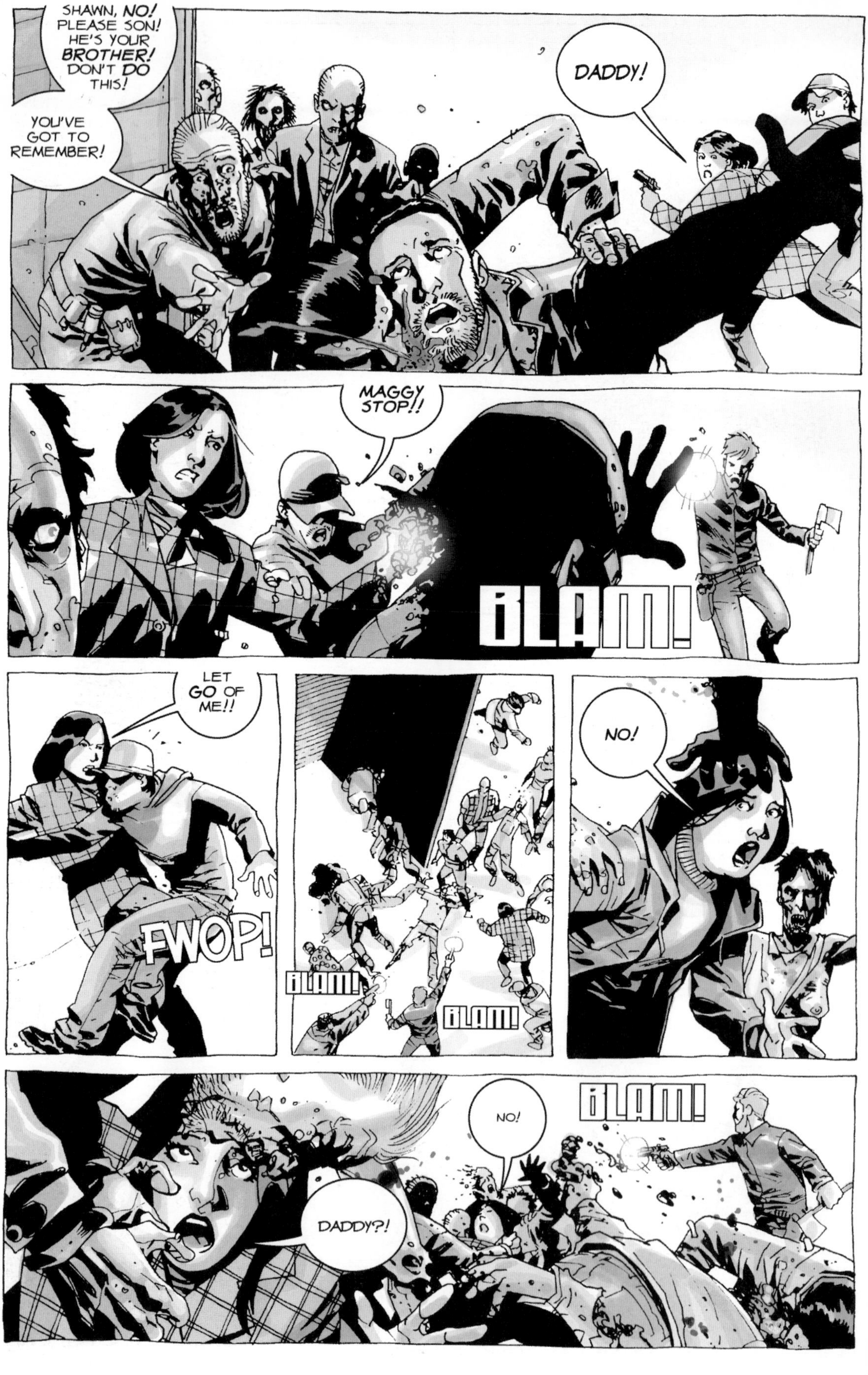
SHAWN, NO! PLEASE SON! HE'S YOUR BROTHER! DON'T DO THIS!
YOU'VE GOT TO REMEMBER!
DADDY!
MAGGY STOP!!
BLAM!
LET GO OF ME!!
FWOP!
BLAM!
BLAM!
NO!
NO!
BLAM!
DADDY?!

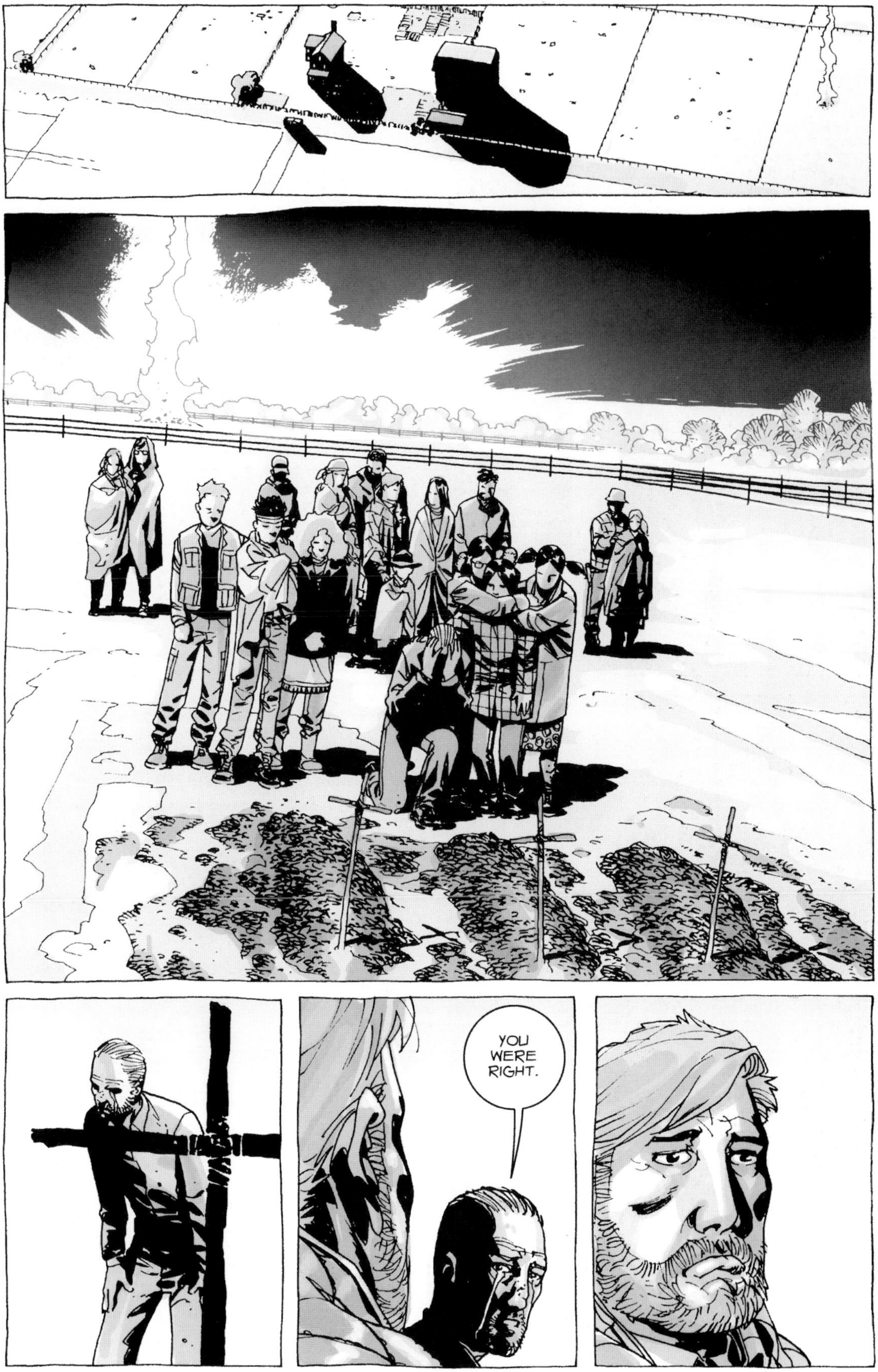
YOU WERE RIGHT.

DAD. MISTER *GRIMES* NEVER TOOK OUR GUNS BACK AFTER TARGET PRACTICE. I DON'T WANT YOU TO GET *MAD* AT US FOR STILL HAVING THEM LATER... SO WE'RE GIVING THEM TO *YOU.*

RICK'S HAD A LOT ON HIS HANDS TODAY, JULIE. I'LL JUST--

YOU KNOW WHAT? HOLD ONTO THEM. YOU'LL BE *SAFER* WITH THEM. I JUST DON'T WANT TO SEE THEM OUT UNLESS IT'S AN *EMERGENCY,* KEEP THEM HOLSTERED AT *ALL* TIMES.

OKAY.

FINALLY. I THOUGHT THAT *BASTARD* WOULD *NEVER* LET US HAVE GUNS.

IT'S GOING TO BE SO MUCH *EASIER* NOW.

YES. WE'LL DO IT AS SOON AS THE TIME IS RIGHT. I *LOVE* YOU, CHRIS.

I LOVE YOU, TOO.

MORNING, HON'.

YOU SLEEP OKAY? I GOTTA SAY... THIS BED IS *REALLY* DOING WONDERS FOR ME. EVEN WITH ALL *THREE* OF US SQUEEZING INTO IT, I'M SLEEPING BETTER THAN I HAVE IN--

YOU OKAY?

NO. MORNING SICKNESS... IT'S COMING AT ME *FULL FORCE* TODAY. I DON'T--

=*ULP!*=

MOM THROWING UP AGAIN?

YEP.

OH.

DALE? YOU COMING?

YEAH, IN A MINUTE. I JUST WANTED TO CLEAN UP A LITTLE. REMEMBER WHEN THIS WAS *OUR* PLACE--BEFORE EVERYONE *ELSE* STARTED SLEEPING IN HERE? THAT WAS *NICE.*

I DON'T THINK I'M *EVER* GOING TO GET THE *SMELL* OUT OF IT. I THINK IT'S SEEPED INTO THE *WALLS.* THIS PLACE IS A *WRECK.*

ERMA WOULD THROW A *FIT* IF SHE COULD SEE IT.

I'M *SORRY.* I KNOW YOU DON'T LIKE IT WHEN I MENTION *HER.*

NO. SHE WAS YOUR *WIFE.* I *UNDERSTAND.* IT'S JUST THAT IT REMINDS ME THAT SHE'S ALWAYS ON YOUR MIND, AND I--

DON'T THINK OF IT THAT WAY, ANDREA. I WAS MARRIED TO ERMA FOR ALMOST *FORTY* YEARS. YOU CAN'T BE JEALOUS OF MY *MEMORIES.*

I *KNOW,* DALE... I *KNOW.*

I *LOVE* YOU, ANDREA. I *REALLY* LOVE YOU.

I *SWEAR.*

I DON'T THINK THIS IS A ONE DAY JOB. NOT BY A *LONG SHOT.* I'M SORRY, MAN--BUT I THINK YOU'VE GOT A *FEW* MORE NIGHTS IN THE *RV.*

LOOKS THAT WAY TO ME TOO. ALTHOUGH, KNOWING THAT I'LL BE OUT OF THAT PLACE *SOON* WILL KEEP ME GOING. IT'LL BE GOOD TO KNOW I'VE GOT A PILE OF HAY WAITING TO REPLACE MY SPOT ON THE *FLOOR* IN FRONT OF THE COUCH.

HANG IN THERE, *BUDDY.* WE'LL HAVE THIS BARN CLEAN IN A FEW *YEARS...*

HEY *ALLEN,* HOW YOU DOING?

YOU *OKAY?*

NO, RICK--AND I PROBABLY NEVER *WILL* BE, BUT THAT'S *OKAY.* I'M KEEPING IT TOGETHER, FOR *DONNA,* FOR THE *KIDS.* THAT'S WHAT SHE WOULD HAVE *WANTED.*

Y'KNOW--DONNA WAS EIGHT YEARS *OLDER* THAN ME. SHE WAS *ALWAYS* WISER--MORE LEVEL-HEADED... SHE ALWAYS KNEW WHAT TO DO, OR WAS ABLE TO *CONVINCE* ME THAT SHE *DID.* I DON'T KNOW *HOW* I'M GOING TO SEE THOSE BOYS TO ADULTHOOD *WITHOUT* HER. I REALLY DON'T KNOW *WHAT* I'M GOING TO DO. BUT I'M GOING TO *TRY.*

I'M GOING TO DO MY BEST.

FOR *HER.*

HERSHEL?

YOU GOT A MINUTE?

LONG AS WHAT YOU'RE ABOUT TO SAY CAN BE SAID IN FRONT OF A *HORSE*, I'M ALL EARS.

HERSHEL. I KNOW IT'S NOT THE BEST TIME TO BE BRINGING THIS UP-- WITH WHAT HAPPENED *YESTERDAY* AND ALL, BUT I WAS THINKING...

ALLEN AND I ARE BACK THERE CLEANING OUT THE *BARN* SO WE CAN *SLEEP* IN IT AND I JUST DON'T SEE THE *POINT* OF IT ALL. WE AIN'T SLEEPING IN THE BARN *FOREVER* AND IF THERE'S EXTRA ROOM IN YOUR *HOUSE* NOW I DON'T SEE WHY WE CAN'T--

NO. ABSOLUTELY *NOT.* YOU'RE *WELCOME* HERE WHILE YOUR BOY *HEALS.* WHEN *HE'S* DONE, *YOU* GO. YOU'RE NOT *MOVING* IN HERE. YOU'RE *NOT* TAKING MY SONS' *ROOM.*

NO.

WHAT?

NO.

NOW LEAVE ME *ALONE.*

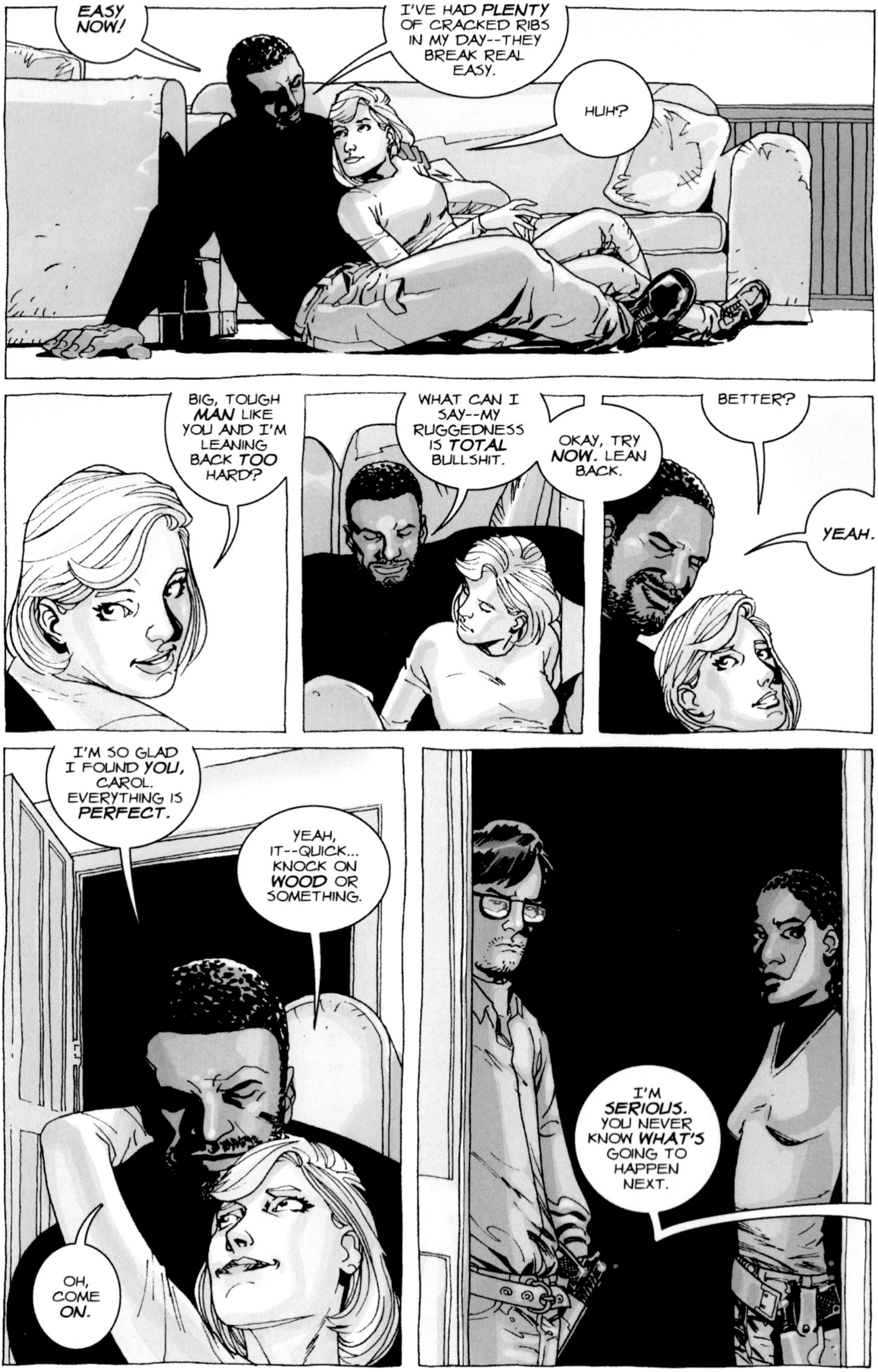
EASY NOW!
I'VE HAD PLENTY OF CRACKED RIBS IN MY DAY--THEY BREAK REAL EASY.
HUH?
BIG, TOUGH MAN LIKE YOU AND I'M LEANING BACK TOO HARD?
WHAT CAN I SAY--MY RUGGEDNESS IS TOTAL BULLSHIT.
OKAY, TRY NOW. LEAN BACK.
BETTER?
YEAH.
I'M SO GLAD I FOUND YOU, CAROL. EVERYTHING IS PERFECT.
YEAH, IT--QUICK... KNOCK ON WOOD OR SOMETHING.
OH, COME ON.
I'M SERIOUS. YOU NEVER KNOW WHAT'S GOING TO HAPPEN NEXT.

LORI-- *DON'T!*

HEY!

YOU'RE THROWING US OUT?! *WHY?! WHAT THE HELL* DID WE *DO*, DAMMIT?!

HOW CAN YOU LET US STAY HERE FOR *WEEKS* AND THEN JUST TURN US *AWAY?*

I NEVER *INVITED* YOU TO *LIVE* HERE. I'M LETTING YOU *STAY* HERE WHILE YOUR SON *HEALS.* I DON'T HAVE ENOUGH FOOD TO FEED *ALL* OF US LONG-TERM. I HAVE TO LOOK OUT FOR MY *FAMILY.*

YOU MEAN BY KEEPING A DAMN *BARN FULL* OF *ZOMBIES* NEXT DOOR?! OR DO YOU MEAN YOU'RE GOING TO START LOOKING OUT FOR YOUR FAMILY FROM *NOW* ON?

IF WE HADN'T BEEN HERE--AND GIVEN YOU OUR EXTRA *GUNS*--YOU'D *ALL* BE *DEAD* RIGHT NOW! BUT YOU'RE GOING TO *KICK US OUT?*

WHAT DO YOU *WANT* FROM ME? I SAVED YOUR BOY'S *LIFE* AND I *LOST* TWO OF MY *OWN.* HAVEN'T I GIVEN YOU *ENOUGH?!*

WE DIDN'T *KILL* YOUR KIDS--IF *ANYONE* HERE IS RESPONSIBLE FOR THAT IT'S *YOU* AND YOUR *STUPIDITY!*

YOU'VE RUN YOUR MOUTH *ENOUGH*, WOMAN!

DAD, NO!

THAT'S ENOUGH!

DON'T YOU *FUCKING* TOUCH *ME!*

YOU WERE GOING TO *HIT* ME?! WHAT THE FUCK IS *WRONG* WITH YOU?!

I LOST *THREE* KIDS YESTERDAY, YOU STUPID *BITCH! THREE!* TODAY I FIND ONE OF YOU *FUCKING MY DAUGHTER*--THEN YOUR *HUSBAND* IS ASKING TO TAKE MY KIDS' *ROOMS!* AND NOW YOU'RE ON MY ASS BECAUSE I WON'T LET YOU *FREE-LOADERS EAT* ALL MY *DAMN FOOD* AND FILL UP MY *HOUSE!*

WHERE THE *HELL* DO YOU GET OFF?! THIS IS *MY FUCKING* HOUSE. I HAVE A *FAMILY* TO LOOK AFTER. I DON'T OWE YOU *SHIT!*

I DON'T OWE YOU SHIT.

WE NEVER SAID YOU *DID*, HERSHEL.

WE *THOUGHT* YOU WERE LETTING US *STAY* HERE. YOU *NEVER* MENTIONED THIS BEING *TEMPORARY*, *GODDAMN* IT.

DO YOU HAVE *ANY* IDEA WHAT IT'S *LIKE* OUT THERE? *HUNTING* FOR *FOOD?* CRAMMING INTO THAT FUCKING *RV?* GETTING ATTACKED BY THOSE *MONSTERS* AT EVERY *GODDAMN* TURN?

NOT.

MY.

PROBLEM.

I'VE GOT TO LOOK OUT FOR MY *KIDS.*

WHAT ABOUT *OUR* KIDS?

YOU'VE GOT A *FENCE--A HOUSE--*YOU'RE *SAFE* HERE. WE COULD HELP YOU GROW *MORE* FOOD IN THE SUMMER, WE COULD MAKE IT *WORK!*

WE COULD HAVE A *LIFE* HERE. YOU CAN'T JUST SEND US BACK OUT THERE. WE COULD *DIE!* YOU'RE SENTENCING US TO *DEATH!*

YOU CAN'T *DO* THIS!

LORI, *PLEASE.*

IT'S GOING TO BE *OKAY.*

HERSHEL? YOU IN THERE? I WANNA *TALK* TO YOU.

I AIN'T GOT NO *CLUE* WHAT'S RUNNING AROUND IN YOUR HEAD, MAN--BUT YOU COULDA *SHOT* THAT MAN.

YOU *HEAR* ME IN THERE?

MAN, I UNDERSTAND YOU WANTING THEM TO *GO*--BUT THAT AIN'T *NO WAY* TO BE TREATIN' ANYBODY. YOU GOTTA *APOLOGIZE* TO RICK BEFORE HE GOES, MAN.

YOU *GOTTA*--

YOU *IN* THERE?

HERSHEL?

HERSHEL!

I WAS GOING TO *SHOOT* THAT MAN, *OTIS.* I WAS GOING TO PULL THAT *TRIGGER* IF HE RESISTED IN *ANY* WAY. I WANTED THEM TO LEAVE *THAT* BAD.

I *ALMOST* PULLED THE TRIGGER. I ALMOST *KILLED* A MAN.

I THINK I'VE LOST MY MIND.

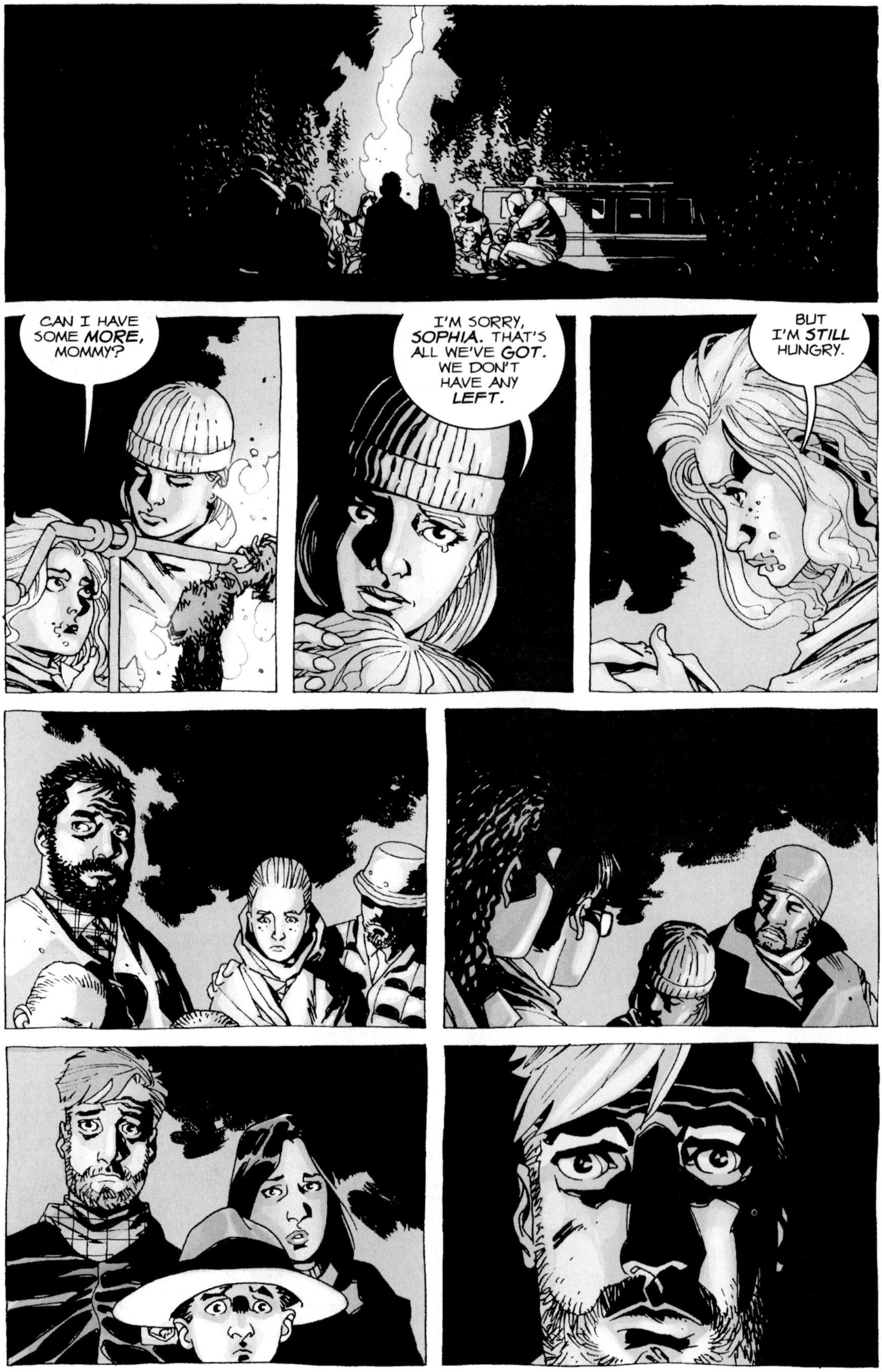
CAN I HAVE SOME MORE, MOMMY?
I'M SORRY, SOPHIA. THAT'S ALL WE'VE GOT. WE DON'T HAVE ANY LEFT.
BUT I'M STILL HUNGRY.

NOTHING?

NOTHING WE CAN EAT.

WE'RE OUT OF *GAS.* WE HAVEN'T SEEN ANY STRANDED CARS FOR A *WHILE.* I WANT EVERYONE TO SPREAD OUT, LOOK FOR CARS, *ANYWHERE.* IF YOU SEE ANY NEARBY HOUSES, LET US KNOW, THERE'S GOT TO BE *SOMETHING* AROUND HERE WE COULD AT LEAST SPEND A *FEW* NIGHTS IN TO GET OUT OF THE RV.

KEEP YOUR GUNS HANDY. IF YOU SEE ANY *ZOMBIES,* DON'T LET YOURSELF GET *SURROUNDED.* DON'T FORGET, WE'RE SMARTER *AND* FASTER. *DON'T* LOSE YOUR COOL. *RUN* IF YOU HAVE TO.

IF YOU FIND ANY *FOOD...* BRING IT BACK SO WE CAN *SHARE* IT. REMEMBER THE *KIDS.*

IF YOU FIND *ANYTHING,* FOOD, GAS, WATER, OR SHELTER, COME BACK TO THE RV AND HONK THE *HORN. ALLEN* WILL BE HERE WITH THE *KIDS.*

IF YOU DON'T FIND ANYTHING, BE BACK HERE BEFORE *DARK.*

WE'VE ONLY GOT A *FEW* HOURS.

FINALLY, ALONE TIME.

DON'T GET ANY IDEAS. I'M *STARVING.* WE'RE NOT DOING *ANYTHING* UNTIL WE FIND SOME *FOOD.*

IF I COULD GET AWAY WITH IT... I'D GNAW A PIECE OFF OF *YOU.*

FUNNY GIRL.

YOU *KIDS* THESE DAYS--I JUST DON'T *GET* YOUR HUMOR.

UH-HUH.

ANOTHER DAY WITHOUT FOOD AND *NONE* OF US WILL BE LAUGHING.

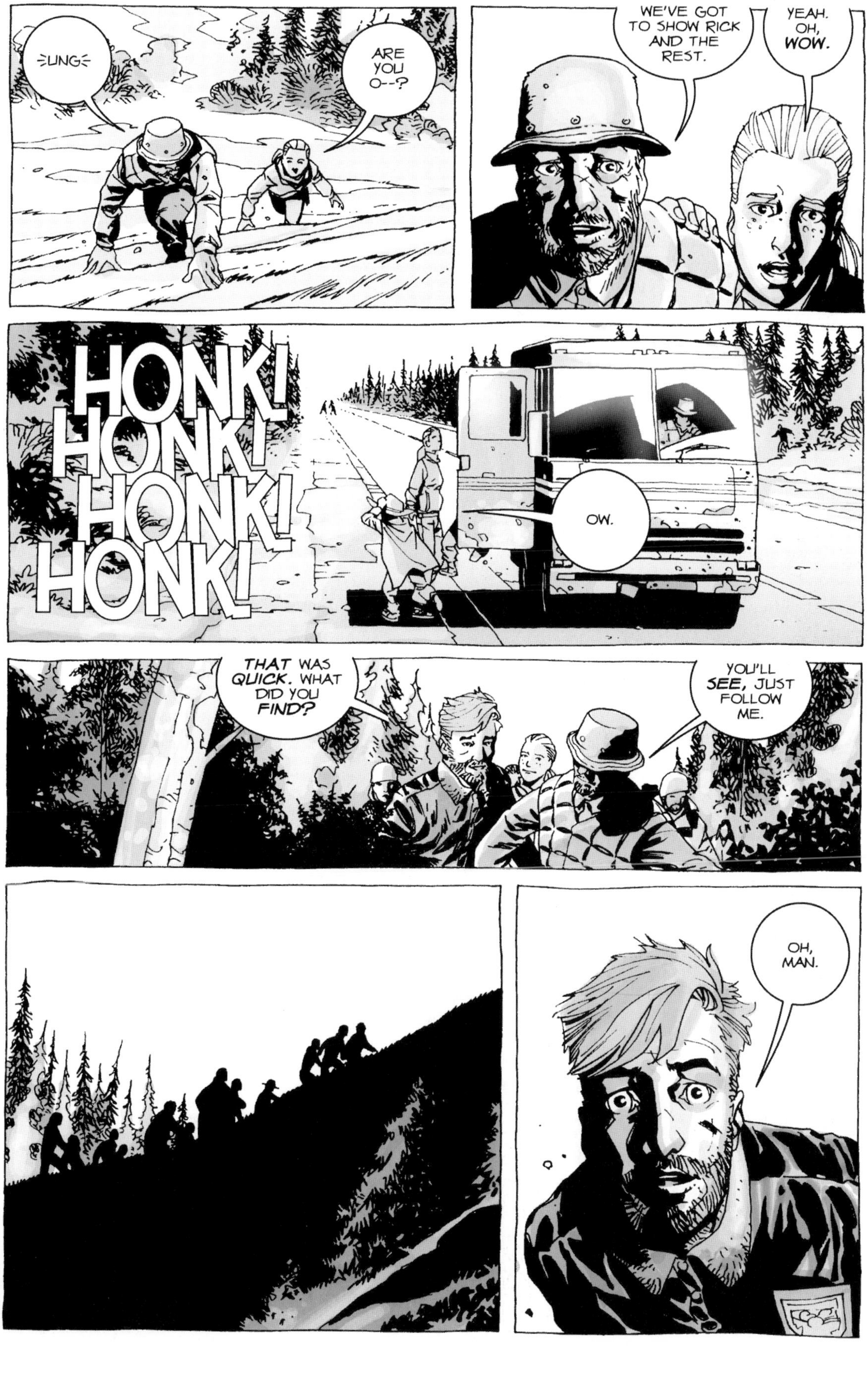

UNG
ARE YOU O--?
WE'VE GOT TO SHOW RICK AND THE REST.
YEAH. OH, WOW.
HONK! HONK! HONK! HONK!
OW.
THAT WAS QUICK. WHAT DID YOU FIND?
YOU'LL SEE, JUST FOLLOW ME.
OH, MAN.

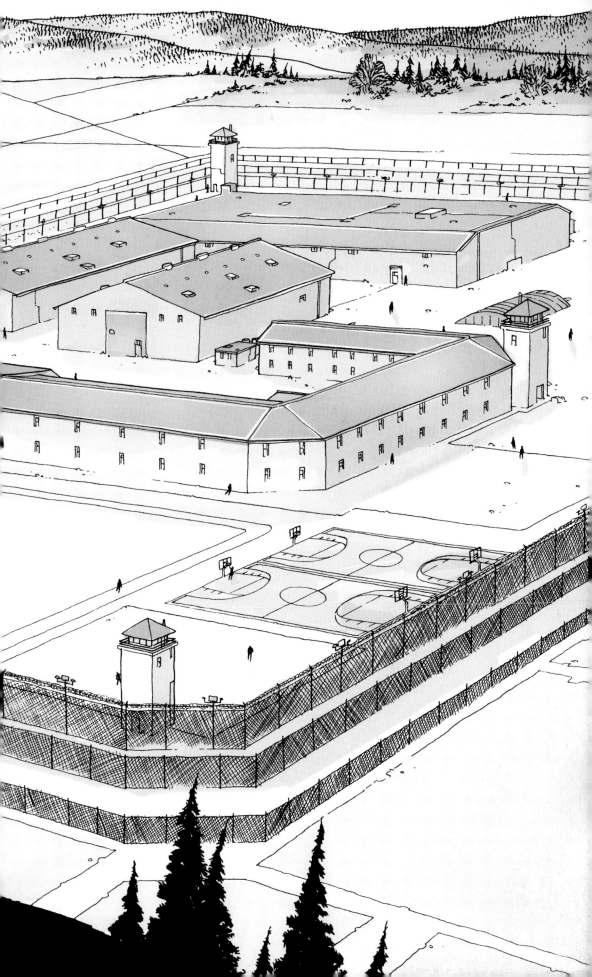

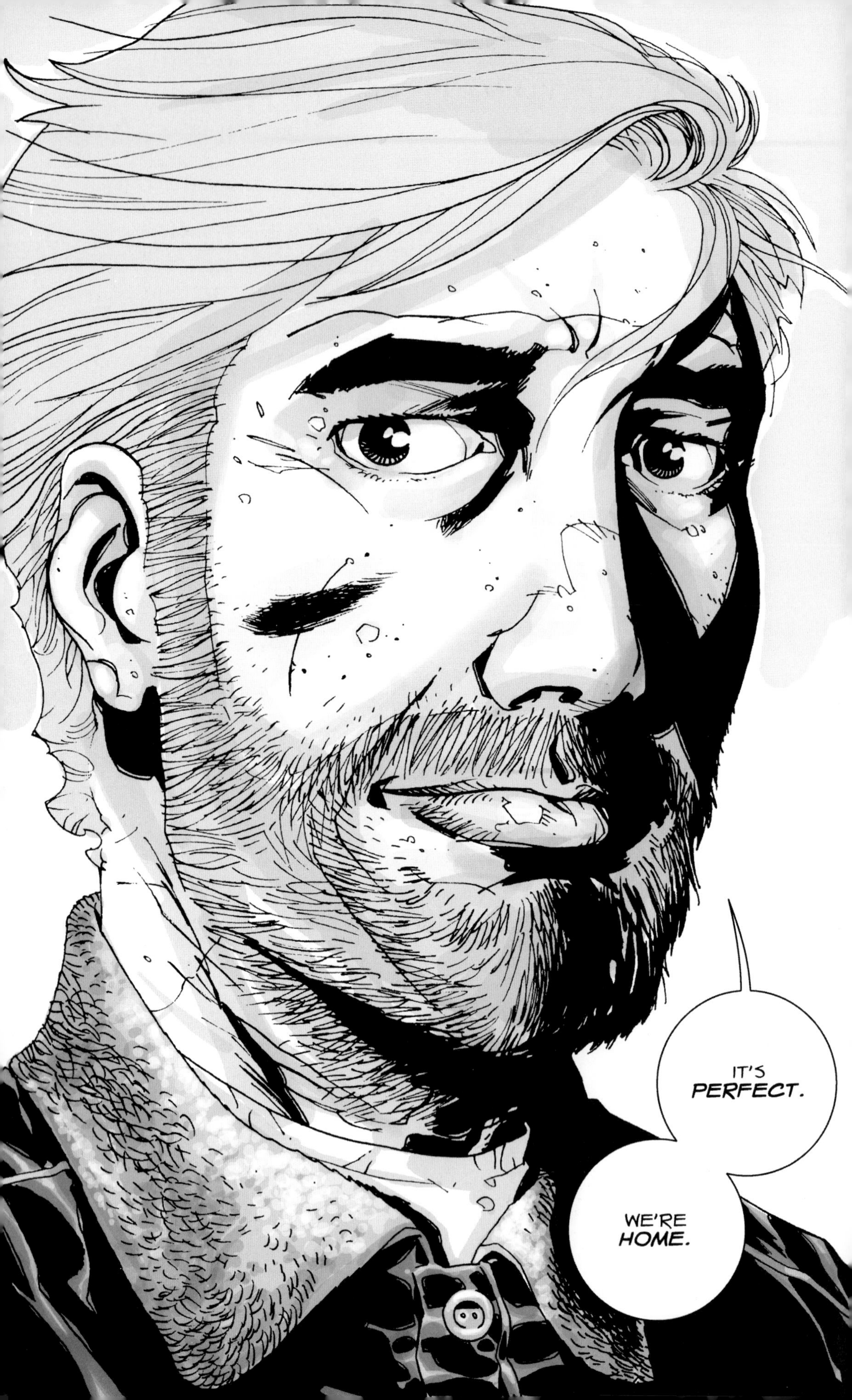
IT'S PERFECT.
WE'RE HOME.

AFTERWORD BY SIMON PEGG

While other monsters clamour for attention with capes and claws and bandages, the zombie has embedded itself into our consciousnesses with little more that a stumble and a moan. Metaphorically, this classic creature embodies a number of our greatest fears. Most obviously, it is our own death, personified. The physical manifestation of that thing we fear the most. More subtly, the zombie represents a number of our deeper insecurities. The fear that deep down, we may be little more than animals, concerned only with appetite. Zombies can represent the threat of collectivism against individuality. The notion that we might be swallowed up and forgotten, our special-ness devoured by the crowd.

Oddly, those rotten bastards also give us hope. The undead maybe tenacious, single minded and as relentless as lava, but they are also stupid and slow; ineffectual and inept. You don't have to be Van Helsing, or even Peter Venkman to throw down with a zombie. Anyone with a pulse can step up. As long as you keep your head, defeating a zombie is not an insurmountable task. You don't need spells, or stakes, or silver bullets, you just need your wits and a weapon. A gun is good, but most blunt objects will do, things we might have around the house or the garden. It is perhaps this combination of hope in the face of terror, that makes the zombie so attractive to us. The idea that we could ourselves, beat death. Beat it until its brains come out of its ears.

With The Walking Dead, Robert Kirkman has brilliantly captured the spirit of George A. Romero's definitive vision of the modern zombie and applied it to his own epic tale of survival. I would imagine everybody reading this has at some time or another asked themselves the question: What would I do? How would I survive if it was me against them? Whilst our favourite zombie movies always seem to finish far too quickly, leaving us wondering what happened next, Kirkman is able to savour the journey and explore the many dangers and dilemmas facing his increasingly diminishing and outnumbered band of survivors. Often, as in some of the best zombie stories, the ghouls themselves are merely bit part players, a context in which to play out the human story. Our real concerns are for the people that remain, for their future and by proxy, our own.

The Walking Dead brilliantly captures the simple truth that in the face of Armageddon, the little things remain unchanged. We still love and hate the same people. We still like the same bands, get the horn, remain frightened of heights and spiders. Kirkman cleverly focuses his narrative on the enduring minutiae of human existence and uses a full blown zombie apocalypse to bring it into sharp relief. Often the roots of great fantasy are firmly embedded in the truth. It is this simple reality that makes The Walking Dead such an engrossing read.

Now, that may be just be a load of bullshit, film school speculation, but as we all know, it's unwise to underestimate a zombie. So if you're a fan who's just torn through this volume, devouring it hungrily, clawing at each page turn, desperate for the next morsel of information, go back to the beginning, take a big deep breath and start again. Savour it, think about it, re-evaluate it and like the best zombies, take it slow.

Simon Pegg
2004

MORE GREAT TITLES FROM
ROBERT KIRKMAN & IMAGE

BRIT
ISBN# 1-58240-385-6
PRESTIGE FORMAT
$4.95

BRIT: COLD DEATH
ISBN# 1-58240-386-4
PRESTIGE FORMAT
$4.95

BRIT: RED WHITE BLACK & BLUE
ISBN# 1-58240-378-3
PRESTIGE FORMAT
$4.95

**INVINCIBLE, VOL. 1:
FAMILY MATTERS**
ISBN# 1-58240-320-1
TRADE PAPERBACK
$12.95

**INVINCIBLE, VOL. 2:
EIGHT IS ENOUGH**
ISBN# 1-58240-347-3
TRADE PAPERBACK
$12.95

**INVINCIBLE, VOL. 3:
PERFECT STRANGERS**
ISBN# 1-58240-391-0
TRADE PAPERBACK
$12.95

**TECH JACKET, VOL. 1:
LOST AND FOUND**
ISBN# 1-58240-314-7
TRADE PAPERBACK
$12.95

REAPER
ISBN# 1-58240-354-6
GRAPHIC NOVEL
$6.95

**THE WALKING DEAD, VOL. 1
DAYS GONE BYE**
ISBN# 1-58240-358-9
TRADE PAPERBACK
$9.95

*For The Comic Shop Near You Carrying Comics And Collections From Image Comics,
Please Call Toll Free 1-888-Comic Book.*